GOD
Incidents III

GOD
Incidents III

More True Stories of God Working
In the Lives of Catholics

Thomas R. Lukes

ISBN-13: 978-0-578-89735-6
Library of Congress Control Number: 2017909756

Cover design: Stephen R. Lukes, graphic & industrial designer
Cover Image: *Red Sky* by William Cather Hook

Printed in the United States of America

This book is dedicated to our

Blessed Mother

Contents

Preface

———•———

I T IS QUITE AMAZING WHAT has happened because of writing this series of *GOD Incidents* books. Not only have I been blessed to hear these stories, but so many readers have told me what a blessing these stories are in their lives.

I have heard of Catholic Bible study groups and Catholic book clubs that have used the books to share as a discussion starter and even families that have read the books together at home. I was told by a *Relevant Radio*® host who interviewed me for his show that he read *GOD Incidents II* three times and can't wait for *GOD Incidents III* to come out.

But there is another side of this book series that should be mentioned: God is revealing His love through these simple and often miraculous stories.

As a result of being a guest on *Relevant Radio* on several occasions, I have had storytellers contact me to share their story;

I have been given the opportunity to interview storytellers from New York, Virginia, Pennsylvania, Illinois, Wisconsin, and Arizona. By talking to these distant storytellers, like John Candela in the borough of Queens, NY, or Barbara Cesarec in Milwaukee, WI, I find that we are united as Catholics who each encounter God in a different way, but His love for us shines through any differences.

I come away from these phone interviews deeply touched and often see insights in the way God works that may have been even overlooked by the storyteller. Jeff Vespalec from West Bend, WI, said about his story, "Reading this helps me to see a little clearer how God has been part of my life, even when I did not know it."

I think that this is a common feeling. The story that was planned to be shared frequently had other parts to it that were not clear until the whole story was put together. I really believe that we take so many events for granted as just coincidences, though if you are willing to give God the credit, you can easily see God's hand in it. They are "God incidents."

I have also tried to give you, the reader, a picture of the family life that often influenced the storytellers not only in their story but how they were raised as Catholics, so you too can get to know them as your brothers and sisters in Christ.

This is the third book in the series. I must thank all the wonderful people who have been willing to step forward and share their stories with a complete stranger and often from another part of the country. I must admit I have come to know these storytellers in a profound way—a sense that I am united with them through Christ for a common purpose to tell what God has done in their lives. When you read the stories in *GOD Incidents III*, notice how many different parts of the country the readers are from and notice how diverse the stories are.

Remember *God loves you and there is nothing you can do about it*, except to embrace His love and turn ever more to Him, with Mary as a source for growing closer to Him through the rosary. (My wife, Lois, and I say a rosary every day that includes a long list of intentions, so try saying the rosary as a couple or as a family and you will find peace and a new closeness to God.)

Thomas R. Lukes

Thomas R. Lukes

Introduction

By John Harper Host/Managing Editor,
Morning Air®, *Relevant Radio®*

"WHAT A COINCIDENCE." YOU'VE PROBABLY said that many times when something fortuitous happened in your life. So, did I. Until I met Tom Lukes.

Those coincidences you're probably replaying in your mind didn't just happen. They are true God incidents. You might have given a wink and a nod to God when you got out of a tight situation. But, as person of faith, you and I can replay those moments in our lives and see the powerful hand of the Holy Spirit at work. The spiritual dots connect. We see the providential hand of God in those moments in our lives.

These God incidents though aren't just fond memories upon which we can reflect. As you'll read in this book, these God incidents represent those powerful moments that remind us that God is in charge. They remind us of His unending love for us, that *He wants only the best for us.*

The stories you'll read are more than just a compilation of events where people simply navigated through the circumstances in their lives with the help of God. In a way, Tom's book will inspire you to do an examination of conscience. Did you trust God as He took you down a path you didn't anticipate? You'll read stories of trust and hope, sometimes hope restored when there was little present. And how many times have we been there? Through the experiences of others, you'll see those moments in your life that were God incidents You'll remember the graces God gave you in those moments where God was present when you needed Him most.

Tom Lukes may have the longest running series of books on one topic since the invention of the printing press! There always will be God incidents in our lives. We just must hope and trust in Him as He takes us on His route—not ours—on the path to Heaven.

Tom's first appearance on the *Morning Air* program on Relevant Radio was a true God incident. His stories of God incidents inspired the Relevant Radio listeners who shared their stories, many of which you'll read in Tom's books. The Holy Spirit will be at work when you read these stories and remind you of your own God-incidents . . . which probably will be in Tom's *next* book!

CHAPTER 1

From Argentina with Love

———•———

Story from Elena d'Autremont of St. Cyril of Alexandria Church in Tucson, AZ

> *Whoever eats my flesh and drinks my blood has eternal life and I will raise him up on the last day.*
>
> JOHN 6:54

BUENOS AIRES IS THE CAPITAL of Argentina on the southeast part of South America. Argentina was established in 1536, but over the centuries that followed, it was settled primarily by Italians and Spaniards.

This is where Elena Bellizzi was born, the second child in the family. She came from a strong Catholic family who instilled their *love of God* in her. She attended Catholic schools and in high school was taught by an order of nuns, who she said were "the female equivalent of the Jesuits." This Catholic education from her early childhood provided her with a solid foundation for her faith. As Elena put it, "Throughout my life, I never doubted God."

When she was in her mid-twenties, she spent a summer in Colorado on scholarship studying under Wilbert E. Moore, a well-known sociologist. It was her stay in Denver that changed her life forever. That is where she met Charles d'Autremont, the owner of a river rafting company.

When they met, it was "love at first sight" for both. She never dreamed that she would meet someone in Colorado with whom she would fall in love and marry. But this was God's plan for Elena and Charles. They have now been married forty-six years.

Charles' family was not Catholic. In fact, they were a real mixture of faiths. They consisted of a devout Unitarian grand-mother, cousins who were Jehovah Witness, Sikhs, Catholics, and even an Episcopalian minister. Charles and his mother, Ann, were both nonpracticing Protestants. This was quite a contrast to Elena's family, who had been Catholic for generations.

Their wedding took place in the Basilica del Santísimo Sacra-mento (the Basilica of the Blessed Sacrament) in Buenos Aires. It was the church where Elena's parents were married. It was a beautiful wedding—and a chance for the two families to meet. There was some concern about Elena marrying a non-Catholic, and in fact, she did have to take a firm stance, especially with the Jehovah Witness family member: "I'm Catholic and don't think about changing me."

When their first child was born, he was baptized in the Catholic Church without any objection from Charles's side of the family. However, a few months later, when Charles's sister had her first child baptized in the First Church of Christ in Sandwich, Massachusetts, a slight conflict arose.

Elena's mother-in-law, Ann, suggested to Elena and Charles that they should also have their son baptized in that church. Fortunately, the minister said, "Mrs. Dearborn, I am sure that one baptism is enough for this child." His words of wisdom helped to avoid a potential family dispute without any involvement of either parent.

Years later, Ann, who lived in Massachusetts, traveled to Europe, where she was very moved by the city of Assisi, Italy. As gifts to Elena, she brought back a beautiful decorative antique pendant and a framed copy of the "Prayer of St. Francis."

It seemed from that time forward, Ann was much more accepting of Elena as her Catholic daughter-in-law. Perhaps the history that surrounded the birthplace of St. Francis (1181–1226) spoke of the longevity of the Catholic Church to Ann.

Over the years, there were plenty of times when Elena, Charles, and their three children spent time with their grandmother on the East Coast. Later in her life, Grandma Ann became ill. By this time, Elena and the family had moved to Tucson, Arizona.

One day, Elena entered her parish church for weekday Mass, wearing the pendant that Ann had given her. As soon as she entered the church, she began to cry uncontrollably—"sadness overwhelmed me." She could not control her sobbing. Embarrassed, Elena continued to pray and do her best to suppress the crying. When she arrived home, she received a phone call informing her that Ann had died. She thought: "I had no idea why I was overtaken with grief at St. Cyril's Church, but now I know, it was for Ann."

Raising three children meant that Elena had a busy schedule to juggle. After dropping off the children at school, her weekly routine included attending weekday Mass at St. Cyril's. Afterward, as an "extraordinary minister[1] of the Eucharist,"[2] she would take a Pyx (pronounced "pix")[3] with consecrated hosts to the sick at the Tucson Medical Center (TMC).

TMC was a large hospital with different wings for different levels of care. When a patient was admitted to the hospital, they would be asked their religious faith. A priest would drop by those patients who were more seriously sick and Catholic. He would administer the sacrament of the sick, hear confession,[4] and offer Holy Communion; while Elena, as an extraordinary minister of the Eucharist, would pray with those less seriously sick and offer them Holy Communion.

Elena would introduce herself and ask if the patient would like to receive the Eucharist. Sometimes they would say, "No, I need to go to confession first." Elena would then make a notation for the priest to stop by to hear their confession. If they said "Yes," she would say an Our Father with them and give them Holy Communion from her pyx.

She was never directed to the very sick; only the priest would visit them. However, one day, Elena was taken to the wing for the more seriously ill patients. When the two nurses who were leading her stopped at the first patient's room, she was told that there was no reason for her to go in, because the woman in that room had been in a coma for more than a week. Elena responded, "I can at least pray for her." She entered, followed by the two nurses.

Elena went over to the woman, who appeared to be unconscious. Elena put her hand lightly on her arm and began saying the Our Father in a soft voice. Halfway through the prayer, the woman opened her eyes. Elena, instead of being shocked, told the woman that she was from St. Cyril's Church offering Eucharist to the sick. "Would you like to receive Holy Communion?" The woman said yes, so Elena opened the pyx and gave her a Host. Immediately, the woman said, "Jesus, Jesus, Jesus" with joy and delight. Elena described the woman's reaction as if she had been surprised to meet an old friend after years apart. Afterward, they spoke briefly, but after a few minutes, the woman closed her eyes and went back into a coma.

When the woman slipped back into unconsciousness, Elena and the nurses looked at each other. What had they just witnessed: a moment of clarity, just long enough to receive Holy Communion and drift back into sleep!

The woman's response to receiving Holy Communion—calling out the name of Jesus, as if she was in His presence, was even more of a surprise than her suddenly awakening from the coma.

It also confirmed Elena's belief in *the Real Presence of Jesus* in the Eucharist, while for the nurses it certainly must have raised questions in their minds about the Catholic faith.

———•———

[1] **An extraordinary minister of the Eucharist** is a lay person who is specially appointed by the pastor to assist with the distribution of Holy Communion at Mass or to the sick who are unable to go to Mass.

[2] **Eucharist** refers to both the Mass that is the liturgy celebrated daily in the Catholic Church and to the bread and wine that Catholics believe becomes the Body and Blood of Christ when the priest says the words of consecration. Catholics believe this because of what Jesus said in the Gospel of John chapter 6 and what Paul wrote 1 Corinthians 11:27–29.

These passages make clear that Jesus meant what He said in Jn 6:53, "Unless you eat the flesh of the Son of Man and drink his blood, you do not have life within you." This is why the Eucharist is the core of the liturgical celebration and why the Mass is also called the "Liturgy of the Eucharist."

The Greek word based in ecclesiastical Greek *eukharistia* meaning "thanksgiving" or "giving thanks." The Early Church Fathers (St. Ignatius 88–110 AD, St. Justin Martyr 100–165 AD, and many others) all spoke of the Eucharist as the actual Body and Blood of Christ. It was not until the Protestant Reformation in 1517 that the Protestants rejected this idea.

Catholics use "Holy Communion" interchangeably with "Eucharist."

[3] **Pyx** is a small round vessel in which the Sacred Host is either preserved or carried. It is made of precious metal, gold or silver, and if made of silver, it is usually gold-plated. The ciborium is the ordinary receptacle for the preservation of the Sacred Host in the tabernacle. A smaller pyx is used for carrying the Blessed Sacrament to the sick. It holds one to four or five Hosts.

[4] **Confession (**or Reconciliation) is a sacrament performed only by a priest in *"Persona Christi"* (in the person of Christ), in which the penitent confesses his/her sins to the priest in order to restore their soul to a sinless condition. The Catholic Church has always taught that one cannot receive Holy Communion if they have committed a mortal (grave) sin that has not been confessed to a priest. This also explains, in part, why a non-Catholic cannot receive the Eucharist, since they have never had the opportunity to confess their sins. The other reason is that they are not in communion (in acceptance) w all the Church teachings.

CHAPTER 2

Guardian Angels

———•———

Stories from three listeners on *Relevant Radio*[®1] on *The Drew Mariani Show* and the *Inner Life Show*

> *See that you do not despise one of these little ones,*
> *for I say to you that their angels in heaven always*
> *look upon the face of my heavenly Father.*

MATTHEW 10:18

October 2nd is the feast of Guardian Angels. I happened
to be listening to Relevant Radio and I wanted to share
several of the stories from those two shows.

Storyteller: Susan from Springfield, Oregon

WE ALL HAVE HEARD STORIES about guardian angles, but Susan has had her doubts. After what happened to her one evening, she is now a believer.

It was time to close-up the office when she noticed that the light on the back porch was out. The light provided some security to their office during the night, so she felt it was necessary to do something about it right away.

In the cabinet Susan found a light bulb and grabbed the nearby stool and with those she headed out to the porch. Now, *spontaneous decisions can be deadly.* So, as soon as Susan climbed up on the stool a sense came over her that she shouldn't be up there; but it was clearly too late, since her task was nearly complete, or so she thought. Suddenly, the stool started shaking and she could feel herself beginning to lose her balance. In an instant, she realized that if she fell, she would end up on the ground below the deck and *that would not be good.* Just when Susan knew it was too late, she felt something stop her fall. "I felt someone catch me."

Relieved, she carefully got down from the stool and thanked God for the help of her guardian angel. The replacement of the bulb would have to wait until tomorrow—Susan would ask her husband to replace it, while she held the stool from tipping.

Storyteller: Ron from Phoenix, Arizona

Ron was ready for Christmas, having already wrapped the boys' presents, when he brought his boys home from school. It was only then that the problem was discovered. His oldest boy pointed out to his dad that his bedroom window was broken. This was not good. So, Ron had his boys stay in the car, while he went next door to call the police. (He was concerned that someone was inside his house.)

When the police arrived, they went through the house and told Ron it was safe to enter. He soon discovered that all the Christmas presents had been stolen. He knew that he didn't have enough money to replace them, so he was at a loss to know what to do.

Soon his wife arrived, since it was her weekend to have the boys. After they were gone, Ron headed to church for an adoration hour of prayer. At this point, Ron knew that only God could help, but he didn't know how. He spoke to God about his loss and reminded God that this was his Son's birthday, yet his own boys no longer were going to have any presents. He told God if this is what he wanted, Ron was okay with it.

He said a rosary and finished his hour with God.

He was awakened early the next morning by a knock on his front door. (Ron described himself as a rather "a large burly guy".) He didn't even take time to put a shirt on but opened the door bare-chested standing there in his pajama bottoms. There, holding a box was a young man about seventeen. He didn't seem bothered by Ron's size or appearance, but instead addressed Ron by name, "Mr. Johnson do you believe in Christmas?" (Ron wondered how he knew his name.)

For some reason, Ron immediately thought of a few "smart" answers. Ignoring this impulse, he asked the young man, "What are you selling?" Unfazed, the young man repeated his question, "Do you believe in Christmas?" Finally, Ron gave in and answered, "Yes." With that, he handed Ron the box that he had been holding and turned and walked away.

Once inside, Ron opened the box only to discover that it held a cup filled with rolls of money, each tied with a ribbon. He set down the box and went outside to thank the young man, but he was no longer there. Ron ran out to the street and looked for him. He was gone! So, he ran up and down the street, but nothing.

When his neighbor asked Ron what he was doing, Ron told him he was looking for a young man who had just been at his front door. The neighbor had not seen him.

When Ron went back inside, he took the money out and counted it. He discovered that it came within twenty-five cents of the money he needed to replace the boys' Christmas presents. Ron dropped to his knees and gave thanks to God for sending an angel to help him.

He still has that cup to remind him of that day many years ago.

Storyteller: Jeanne from La Habra, California

Sometimes we try with logic to explain events in our life, but what Jeanne and her husband experienced that day, they could not explain.

Jeanne and her husband found that the trip from Houston to Los Angeles where her dad lived was a long drive to make every month, but they couldn't afford to fly that far monthly. Jeanne's dad was slowly dying.

On this particular trip, they were deep in conversation not paying attention to the amount of gas in the tank. Jeanne saw a sign that said, "Next gas twenty miles," so she looked down and gasped when she saw the gauge on "empty".

They both felt that there was no way that they were going to make it, so they decided to say a Rosary. When they were nearing the end of the Rosary, they noticed an off ramp leading to what appeared to be a small gas station; so, they took it. They both thanked God that they had made it.

The station had only one pump, so they happily filled up the tank, paid the attendant and drove away. What happened next still is hard to grasp. Jeanne looked in the rear-view mirror only to discover that there was no longer a gas station or attendant. There was nothing!

---

[1] **Relevant Radio**® is a Catholic radio network mainly broadcasting talk radio and religious programming. It is the largest Catholic radio network in the United States. There are 185 stations spread throughout thirty-nine states. The Mass, the rosary, and the Chaplet of Divine Mercy are said every day. (Source: Wikipedia) Find a station where you live: https://relevantradio.com/listen/stations/ or you can listen live using the Relevant Radio App at the App Store

CHAPTER 3

"The Catch"

———•———

Story from Greg and Becky Beardsley of San Carlos Cathedral in Monterey, CA

After he had finished speaking,
he said to Simon, 'Put out to deep water
and lower your nets for a catch.'

LUKE 5:4

IT WAS IN THE YELLOW Sea, near Tsingtao, China, on October 31, 1947, that Gregory Beardsley was born. He was born on a Navy hospital ship, the *USS Repose.* He was the third child of Francis Louis and Frances Louise Beardsley. In the following years, the family grew to ten children, three boys and seven girls. In 1960, the family moved to Carmel, California, where Greg's father, Frank, was a Chief Warrant Officer at the Naval Post-Graduate School in nearby Monterey.

When Greg was twelve, his mother died suddenly of a diabetes-induced coma. At the time, Greg's youngest sister, Joanie, was only eight months old. Within a year, Greg's father met a Navy widow, Helen North, who had lost her husband when his plane crashed in Washington State. A year later, their marriage added her four sons and four daughters to the family. In the years that followed, they also had two children of their own, which made for quite a large family of twenty children.

Greg found that Helen was a loving and caring mom, who did all she could to replace his mom, Francis Louise. Since both parents were devout Catholics, all the children attended Catholic schools. It was the parents' goal to see their twenty children become strong in their faith.

In 1965, Helen somehow found time to write a book. It was titled, *Who Gets the Drumstick?* The rights to this book were purchased by a well-known actress named Lucille Ball. The movie titled *Yours, Mine and Ours*,[1] starring Lucille Ball as Helen and Henry Fonda as Frank, brought further attention to the unusual Beardsley family—now they were not only a big family, but they were the focus of a movie. (Greg was a senior in high school when the movie was being filmed.)

With thoughts of the family behind him, Greg was off to the University of San Francisco, where after four years he earned a degree in Economics with a minor in Theology. During his college years, he attended Mass every Sunday, but that all changed when he graduated and moved away from this Catholic university. As Greg put it, "I became a pagan."

Although he never thought of it at the time, parties and drinking soon replaced God in his life. He had spent his first twenty-one years as a faithful Catholic, but said, "I realized that my relationship with God was based on fear of God, not love for God."

This was going to change, but it would take time.

Other interests soon filled the subtle emptiness in Greg's life. He became a real estate agent and avid 49er fan. For the next five years, he lived without experiencing God and His love. *Then he met Becky.*

They dated for two years and were married in 1977. Becky was Catholic but, like Greg, she did not attend church, except for weddings and funerals. They had each other, so they both felt that that was enough. But God had other plans for them.

God's entrance back into Greg's life came in the most unexpected way.

In 1979, the 49ers hired Bill Walsh as their head coach. That year they also drafted Joe Montana from University of Notre Dame as the quarterback of Walsh's "West Coast offense." By 1981, they found themselves in the National League playoff game against the Dallas Cowboys for the right to go to the Super Bowl.

Sitting on the goal line, twenty-two rows up, Greg sat with his father, Frank. Most NFL football fans are very familiar with "the Catch" that clinched the game in the final seconds, but no one knows how it came about. You see, when the 49ers took the ball on the Dallas ten-yard line with two minutes and ninety yards to go, Greg sealed the ultimate win by making a deal with God. He told the God of the universe, who cared little about football, and who had not heard from Greg in more than ten years, that if the 49ers won the game, he would return to the Church.

With less than forty seconds left in the game and the ball on the Dallas twelve-yard line, Joe Montana rolled to his right, chased by two Dallas linemen, and let loose with a perfect spiral. But as Greg thought at the time, "Dwight's not going to catch that ball. It is too high." But somehow Dwight Clark did catch it and the 49ers won!

When asked by the *Sports Illustrated* reporter, "How did you catch it?" Clark replied, "It was over my head. I thought, 'Oh no, I can't go that high.' But something got me up there. It must have been God or something." Greg knew the answer—God had come through for him.

This may appear to most readers as a strange way to return to the Church, but for Greg it didn't matter—a deal was a deal.

He had made a deal with God, now he felt that it was his duty to keep his promise. Greg and Becky returned to church the following Sunday. He enjoyed being there. Soon it became a regular routine. This return to church was not the end, because *love of God* was still not part of Greg and Becky's reason for their return. *Love for God was still coming.*

In 1986, Greg was invited to attend a Christians in Commerce weekend retreat. (I just happened to be there as a participant myself.) It was held at St. Francis Retreat Center high in the hills above the little mission town of San Juan Bautista, California.

The retreat started on Friday night and ended on Sunday afternoon. The series of short talks focused on being a man of God in your prayer life and business. The second day included a time for being prayed over to receive the Holy Spirit.

Greg was very open to this and as he tried to relax, with his eyes closed, is when *it happened.* As he described it, "A huge white light exploded in my head." He felt that someone was shining a high-intensity light in his eyes, but when he opened them, there was nothing to explain his experience.

When Greg returned home on Sunday, "I had a distinct feeling that I was loved by God. I really felt that, like never before." He also had a deep desire to "get into Scripture, and I did." Greg said, "God really poured His grace out on me that weekend."

When Greg returned home, he discovered that Becky had made a wonderful dinner for him that they enjoyed in front of the fireplace. After hearing Greg tell her of his weekend experience, she said, "You have really changed—who is this man?" It was not just what he said to her, but a sense that she had: that *he was different.* Becky made it clear that she was happy for him, but on the other hand, she did not need or want what Greg had experienced. *That too would soon change.*

Also attending the CIC retreat was Denny Powell, who was a member of the "City of the Lord," a charismatic prayer community centered in Arizona. It was six months to a year later that Denny invited Greg and Becky to visit Tempe, Arizona, for the Convocation for the City of the Lord. So, they decided to go.

The convocation could best be described as a high-powered Catholic retreat, complete with speakers, and music with the gifts of the Holy Spirit fully outpoured. Becky said, "During the convocation, the Holy Spirit just came upon me. I fell to my knees crying. I couldn't stop. I cried all the way home on the plane." This awakening continued for three days. Then one night, while in prayer, she received the gift of tongues.

God had brought both Greg and Becky to a deeper relationship with him. As Becky put it, "God just took over." They now walked together deeply in love with God. That emptiness had been filled with joy and the fullness of faith.

When Greg made a deal with God, he had no idea how that would change their lives forever.

NOTE: Since 1986, Greg has continued to be a leader in the Christians in Commerce retreats and Becky has continued to be a loving spouse and prayer-mate of Greg.

---·---

[1] The movie *Yours, Mine and Ours* is still available online.

CHAPTER 4

What Happened?

———•———

Story from Stephen and Beverly Zalan of Our Lady of
Mt. Carmel Catholic Church in Carmel Valley, CA

*"I say to you, rise, pick up your stretcher,
and go home."*

LUKE 5:24

S TEVE WAS SITTING ON THE curb with his head in his
hands. He was not aware that blood covered the back of
his head. Questions filled his confused mind. He really
wasn't sure what had happened. It was all so hard to remember.
He knew he had been jogging, but how did he get here? His
stomach was upset, and his head hurt.

Steve had grown up on the south side of Chicago, where he
had spent the first five years in a Catholic elementary school.
The classes were large, with about fifty kids in each class. The
nuns taught on alternating years with lay teachers.

Later Steve's family moved to a suburb outside Chicago. He attended the public school system, but by then, Steve felt that he had already received a strong Catholic foundation. As Steve put it, "It was the example of the nuns and their loving teaching of the Faith that had a profound impact on me."

Steve's interest in the outdoors and science eventually led him to the University of Chicago and then on to Stanford University for graduate school in geophysics. Steve met his wife, Beverly, in Chicago at the university when they were on a field trip together. They were both studying geophysics.

With both following the same career, they planned to travel outside USA to see other parts of the world and experience other cultures. Upon graduation, they were both hired by Chevron and sent overseas to North Africa.

Even though they were away from the US and in very different cultures, like Nigeria and Angola, they never failed to become part of the local Catholic community. Steve's five years of Catholic elementary school education had long-lasting effects. In 2000, they returned to California and worked at the San Ramon office of Chevron while living in Orinda. This allowed their children to experience four years of high school in the United States.

In 2010, Steve and Beverly retired from Chevron and moved to Monterey, California. They loved Monterey's natural beauty and clean, fresh air. It allowed them to pursue outdoor activities, which included a wide range of exercise. Steve enjoyed setting his alarm for 4:30 a.m., so that he can go on a five-and-a-half-mile run every morning.

In late August 2020, Steve and Beverly were visited by their son-in-law, Alex, from Austin, Texas. He was there to help his mother move to her new residence. The plan for Monday was that Steve and Alex would go kayaking in Monterey Bay at 7:30 that morning. This early time would still give Steve enough time to go for his 6:00 a.m. jog, shower, and have breakfast.

That was the plan, *but this is not what happened.*

Steve left the house a little before 6:00 a.m. on Monday, August 31, for his five-and-a-half-mile run. But at 7:15, Beverly realized that Steve had not returned. She checked the bathroom, only to discover that Steve's towel was still dry, so she knew that he had not slipped into the house unnoticed and showered. Now, she was sure he had not returned home from his run.

She told Alex her concern, grabbed her car keys, and headed out along the Steve's normal route. She told herself that Steve was fine, not to worry, but that really didn't help.

Steve had a routine and he never deviated from it. *What could have happened to him?* After coming to the end of the first leg of his route, she spoke to a neighbor—they had not seen Steve. Turning around, Beverly headed along the second leg of his normal route, her fear mounting. She was relieved when she saw him in the distance sitting on the curb.

She pulled up alongside him, rolled down her window, and asked him what had happened. He replied, "I just felt really sick, and I had to stop."

Beverly described the scene, "At one point he turned his head a little bit and I could see that his head was covered in blood."

She asked, "Oh what happened, did you fall?

Steve said, "No, I didn't."

"Yeah, you did. Let's get you in the car. We're going to the hospital." But Steve insisted that he did not want to go to the hospital. *Beverly realized something was wrong.* He was acting strangely.

Steve didn't have his wallet, which would be needed at the hospital, so she headed home. She hoped that Steve would stop resisting the trip to the hospital—he was stubborn and stronger than she was, but, fortunately, Alex was there to help convince Steve that he had to go.

Beverly could see that Steve was showing signs of hypothermia—she thought he had probably been sitting on the curb in the cool morning for some time, wet from perspiration. She convinced Steve to put on his jacket and she grabbed a blanket to cover his legs, and off they went to the Community Hospital of the Monterey Peninsula.

Because of the COVID 19 virus, all Beverly could do was to escort Steve to the outside check-in at the emergency entrance.

But she was not allowed to go with him into the hospital. It would be one week before she would see her husband again and learn what had happened.

At first, the doctors thought Steve had fallen while jogging—that seemed like the obvious explanation. He had tripped and fallen. The CT scan revealed that Steve not only had a concussion but also had bleeding on his brain from the fall. But no one could explain how he could have fallen on asphalt and not have scrapes on his extremities. Steve himself was not able to help because he remembered nothing of the event or even his encounter with Beverly at the site of the accident.

Because of his condition, Steve was placed in the CDU (clinical decision unit) so that he could be closely monitored. Not only was Steve hooked up to an IV to receive a saline solution, but he was being monitored for oxygen saturation, and heart rhythm, as well as being regularly checked by his nurse because of the head injury.

The breakthrough came, when the cardiologist was visiting Steve in his room. The heart monitor was normal when he arrived, but while he was there, the monitor showed a heart arrhythmia.[1] The doctor told Steve that would explain what happened to him. While jogging, perhaps on a downhill section, he had a severe arrhythmia, which caused him to pass out, falling on his back. By the time he awakened, the concussion had caused the nausea and confusion. The doctor said that he was very lucky that he was not driving a car at the time, because otherwise it could have been fatal.

The cardiologist said that they should be able to operate to fix the point in his heart that had caused the arrhythmia. Arrangements were made for Steve to have the procedure under sedation the next day. The cardiologist used an electric pulse to affect the spot in the heart that caused the problem. Steve was released the following day, much to Beverly's relief.

Once Steve returned home, they reflected on all the elements that had protected Steve from death, truly a "God incident."

- If Steve had been driving a car when this happened, it might have been fatal.
- Alex just happened to be visiting and so he was there to convince Steve to go to the hospital.
- The cardiologist also just happened to be in Steve's room when Steve experienced a mild arrhythmia.
- And finally, Beverly was scheduled to leave the next day to visit their daughter for a week. If Beverly had not been there, Steve would have been sitting on the curb in a daze without anyone to help him.

NOTE: Steve has returned to his normal life, including his morning jog, but for now he is building up to his five-and-a-half-mile distance. He is grateful to be alive. PRAISE GOD!

[1] An arrhythmia is a problem with the rate or rhythm of the heartbeat. During an arrhythmia, the heart can beat too fast, too slowly, or with an irregular rhythm.

CHAPTER 5

Crossing Over

———◆·◆———

Story from Ann Aubrey Hanson of San Rafael Catholic Church,
Rancho Bernardo, California

> *"When you pass through the water,*
> *I will be with you; in the rivers you shall not drown."*

ISAIAH 43:2

THE BLUE SKY SHOWED PROMISE of a beautiful day for a
hike. Two nights in a tent and hiking in the mountains
near Santa Barbara had sounded like a fun way to get
away during spring break. The wildflowers covering the hills
would be a bonus that they looked forward to seeing.

There was a chance of rain, but in California rain was often
just a drizzle and the weatherman was often wrong; after all,
he had said, "A chance of rain."

Best friends Ann and Danica were college seniors at UCSB,
and they really wanted to get away from the stress of classes

and upcoming finals. Danica's mom, Sylvia, was visiting at the time and she was eager to join them, whereas Ann's mom did not want to have anything to do with this backpacking trip. She said, "If God wanted us to sleep outside, he would not have created houses." But she did offer to drive the three of them to the Upper Oso campsite where they would begin their hike. She had promised to return in forty-eight hours to pick them up. (This was before cellphones.)

They said their goodbyes to Ann's mom and walked across the concrete drive that crossed the nearly dry streambed. They stepped over the small rivulet of water and made their way to the other side, following the trail to a picnic area set among the California oak trees.

They began their hike into the hills with anticipation of a fun outing. Ann soon became aware that the hike would be a slow process. She had forgotten that Danica could not walk with any speed; in fact, she had been born with an irregularity of her legs, such that her knees never fully straightened. This forced her to walk slightly bent over and sway with a side-to-side gait. In addition, the trail itself looked dangerous because it was covered with loose rock over adobe, so Danica had to take it even more slowly.

Ann realized that her plan to hike five to six miles the first day was not realistic. However, the slow pace of the hike was not really a problem. It was a beautiful day, and they were out in the fresh air doing exactly what they had planned, just at a slower pace.

Soon the blue sky gave way to gray clouds. They realized that the weatherman might be right after all, but they had come prepared with a rain tarp and a sturdy four-person tent. They had even thought to bring a fold-up shovel to dig a trench around the tent perimeter to protect the tent's interior from the rain.

At about four in the afternoon, a light sprinkling of rain greeted them as they arrived at the second high point of the day's hike, about three miles along the trail. There was a natural flat point just off the trail. Even though Danica wanted to continue, both Sylvia and Ann agreed it was time to set up camp before the rain became heavier. "There's no guarantee we'll find another spot like this," Sylvia said, "and besides, we'd better set up camp before the rain really hits."

They quickly unpacked the camping gear, placed a drop cloth, and staked the tent up over it. While Danica and her mom installed the tent and the secondary rain fly over the tent, Ann dug a trench around the tent perimeter. The sky had darkened as the storm surrounded them.

And then came the rain.

They had been fortunate to have stopped when they did. It was about five o'clock when they zipped up the tent door. The steady rain continued but *without wind*. They tumbled into the tent laughing, figuring they'd caught a break with their campsite, situated as it was on the side of a hill, where no puddles could gather.

Forgoing any thought of a hot meal, they put their backpacks on the leeward side of the tent, downhill, out of the rain and any wind that might arise. It was only five o'clock but the sky had turned black. It didn't matter now—they were dry, snug, and had large rations of drinks and trail mix.

They each climbed into their sleeping bags warm and dry. Their success in quickly setting up the tent and the warmness of their bags offered them a time for reflection and a time to share stories about their lives.

Ann was quite taken aback when Danica shared the story of her own father's death while hiking on a glacier in Alaska with Sylvia, when he fell into a deep crevasse. Sylvia described how she had been forced to climb down to his body to retrieve his backpack, so that she could survive the hike back for help and to later recover his body. Ann was grateful that she had never had to experience anything remotely like that herself.

About eight that evening, the full force of the storm hit with a wind that pounded the rain horizontally against the tent. Exposed as they were high up the mountain, the rain was intense, and it quickly soaked the side of the tent.

They each took turns holding up the tent poles, fearful that the wind would collapse the wet tent on top of them. Water began to flow into the tent, soaking everything. "Moving water flowed across the floor of the tent, sending us into spasms of helpless laughter as peanuts and raisins from the trail mix swirled around our feet." What had just earlier been a time to share stories had turned into a nightmare. Fortunately, their sleeping bags kept them warm and the tent kept them dry.

During the night, the tent could not take the wind any longer and collapsed, with them inside.

"Numb with cold, dripping, and yet somehow still in great humor, we crawled from the collapsed tent at the first sign of light." The heavy rain had subsided, and they had some hope of being able to safely get off the mountain—*they had all had enough. They just wanted to have a hot shower and a warm meal.*

They packed up their water-logged backpacks and got ready to face the muddy trail down to the Upper Oso campsite. It quickly became clear that the condition of the trail would make it impossible for Danica to face the slippery trail while carrying a backpack. Since Sylvia was helping Danica down the trail, she could only deal with her own backpack and still be able to assist Danica.

Ann offered to take Danica's backpack as well as her own, taking one at a time partway down the trail and returning to gather the other backpack and carry it to the next spot. She was able to do this with such speed that she was able to reach the trailhead with both packs before Danica and her mom reached the bottom.

As Ann left the picnic area, she faced a new challenge—the six-inch wide trickle of water in the paved roadway of the streambed was now a raging river some twenty to thirty feet across. Ann realized that Danika would never be able to cross the stream, even with Silvia's assistance, and they wouldn't survive another night with a drenched tent and sleeping bags. Ann left a note on Danica's backpack at the picnic area, letting them know that she was going for help.

With apprehension, she stepped into the water. Halfway across the now-roaring stream, with arms in the air for balance, *she realized that she had made a terrible mistake.*

Not only was the water now up to her waist, but she knew that if she slipped, the heavy backpack would make it impossible to recover her footing. She would surely drown. She called out to God for help. "Lord, I have done a very, very stupid thing here. If I slip, I'm dead. Please give me the strength to get across." With continued prayer, Ann slowly inched her way to the other side of the stream with renewed confidence that she was going to make it.

Once on the other side, Ann walked about a mile to the park fire station where she found help. A fireman drove her back to the river in a massive green pumper truck. They attempted to cross the stream in the truck, but the current was too strong, and he had to back out of the stream onto safe ground.

He turned to Ann and said, "How, little lady, did you ever cross that stream?"

Ann replied, "Only with God's help."

They returned to the fire station, where the fireman radioed for a helicopter to bring Danica and Sylvia out from the park, where they were reunited with Ann.

Note: Ann not only trusted God in her moment of great danger, but at 5'-2" understandably was called "little lady" by the fireman. Ann also was the editor of this book.

CHAPTER 6

Streets of Calcutta

———•———

Story from Dr. Christa Balch of Sacred Heart Catholic Church,
Salinas, CA

The disciples were filled with joy and the Holy Spirit.

ACTS 13:52

*When we yield to God and allow Him to lead us, He
will reveal Himself to us, often in a powerful way.*

CHRISTA KNELT ON THE HARD tile floor in prayer in
front of the altar and tabernacle. The sisters of the
Missionaries of Charity knelt with her in silent prayer.
They prayed for the sick and the dying and for the suffering
people of Calcutta.

Christa grew up in Dana Point, California, with her two sisters,
Cathie and Carrie. Christa was the second child, but she almost
didn't make it because she was born two months premature.

Her mom was so concerned that she would not survive that she decided to name her "Christa." She hoped that by naming her after Christ, He would save her. *It worked,* but along with surviving, she also received the gift of being named Christ or "the anointed." And with His name, God had something special in mind for Christa.

She attended public schools through high school. For her religious education, she received CCD education at their church. As a family, they also faithfully attended Mass on Sunday at St. Edward the Confessor Catholic Church. Her faith foundation was established not only through CCD and church, but through a Catholic family life lived out at home.

It is often impossible to recognize the full impact of a religious education and attendance at church will have on a person.

For Christa, it was at church that she heard a missionary priest speak of *what a blessing it was to be a missionary.* He lit a fire in her heart, even at the early age of thirteen or fourteen. She later learned that to be a "lay missionary," she needed a four-year college degree.

After graduating from high school, Christa went to the University of Santa Barbara, part of the University of California system, to prepare her for her missionary service. She decided to go UCSB because her mom and her grandma had gone there, and the school had an excellent reputation. The four years at the university was a maturing time for Christa.

After graduating from the UCSB with a bachelor's degree in philosophy, Christa went through nine months of training in Los Angeles with the *Lay Mission Helpers*[1] to prepare her for missionary work in Papua New Guinea.[2]

The mission was located on the island of New Britain,[3] which was one of six hundred islands of Papua New Guinea. The missionary complex consisted of a Catholic church, a school, a hospital, and smaller buildings used to house the teachers, nurses, and doctors. Christa lived in a building with the other teachers.

The part of the New Britain Island where the missionary complex was located is called "Vunapope" which means "place of the pope." (Tradition says that the pope had visited there many, many years earlier.) During World War II, Vunapope was held by the Japanese, who destroyed the beautiful Catholic church and for three-and-a-half years kept all the missionaries prisoners.

The existing village was located near the beach at the base of the hill below the missionary complex. It was located right on the Bismarck Sea. The children from the village walked up the hill to school every day.

Over the next three years, Christa experienced a life far removed from what she was used to back in California. Her primary role was as a schoolteacher of the children who lived in the village. The first year she taught fourth/fifth grades; the second year, second/third grades; and the final year, the preschoolers.

The climate was tropical—hot and humid year-round with plenty of rain. Christa was able to get some relief from the heat by scuba diving on her days off. The sea there was part of a coral reef and was filled with colorful fish in the warm waters. It was also full of parts of airplanes and ships—World War II ruins.

The hospital offered medical treatment to the people even beyond the village. Natives walked miles to get to the hospital. It was there that Christa first received her call to become a doctor. She could see that the doctors had a huge healing impact on the people. She wanted that sense of *helping others* in need. It was a call that she was committed to pursue in the years ahead.

When she finished her three-year stay as a missionary in New Britain, she decided to return home by way of India. She wanted to see Mother Teresa's Missionaries of Charity. The motherhouse was in Calcutta, India, so that is where she headed.

She soon discovered that Calcutta was a sharp contrast to Papua, which was more of a rural farm country, whereas Calcutta was a huge metropolis. The population of Calcutta was 14.8 million people—13 percent larger than the entire country of Papua, New Guinea and even larger than New York City.

In Calcutta, poverty was visible in the many sick and dying people in the streets. Families lived in little shacks along the streets, without toilets or running water. The suffering people were quite a shock to Christa. They were everywhere.

For three months, she worked with the sisters of the Missionaries of Charity[4] in the orphanage and the Home for the Sick and Dying. Even though it was emotionally overwhelming, Christa said, "It was a beautiful, wonderful experience."

She would also pray in the chapel with the sisters, kneeling on the hard tile floor. One day while praying, she looked over in the front corner and there was Mother Teresa of Calcutta, later declared a saint in 2008. When she had an opportunity, Christa spoke to Mother Teresa. Mother urged Christa to attend Mass daily. She also told her that if God gave her direction, she should not feel it necessary to seek confirmation from others—she should just follow the Lord's direction.

At one point, she worked in a warehouse that was a home for abandoned baby girls. This was caused by a unique phenomenon to India: baby girls were a problem to a family because it meant that the family would have to come up with a dowry at marriage to give to the groom's family. This led to both abortion and abandonment of girl babies after birth. Christa described the warehouse as having row upon row of cribs, with fifteen cribs in each row. Each crib held three babies. "I'll never forget it. They all wanted to be held." Her role was to pick up a baby for five minutes and hold it as she walked. And then pick another baby and do the same. "It was so sad."

"I also spent a lot of time in my room praying and praying." She found herself praying repeatedly, "Lord, I long to see Your face. Lord, I long to see Your face. Lord, I long to see Your face… Suddenly, *I had this joy come over me*, like I had never experienced in my whole life. I felt His love and His presence."

This feeling of joy was so overwhelming that Christa had to leave the building. She went outside and walked the streets of Calcutta. "I felt overwhelmed by the Holy Spirit." She felt love for every person she saw on her walk. It was as if she saw everyone through the eyes of Christ. She walked for miles in this *state of joy*. Finally, she returned to her room, savoring this profound God incident.

After three months in Calcutta, she returned to Southern California, where she began to pursue her medical degree.

Christa's story continues in the next chapter.

———•———

[1] Lay Mission Helpers was founded in 1955 by Msgr. Anthony Brouwers. LMH provides training and support for lay Catholics who serve three years in mission dioceses around the world. Since its founding, LMH has sent more than 700 single men and women, married couples, and families to serve in thirty-six countries. Teachers, nurses, social workers, computer technicians, administrators, tradesman, and others work together and strive to live a simple life close to the poor. Lay Mission-Helpers serve to share their gifts, live their faith, and learn from one another. Catholic doctors interested in serving in Africa or Latin America can serve with LMH's sister organization, Mission Doctors Association. Source: Wikipedia

[2] Papua New Guinea is part of the large island of New Guinea which is ninety-one miles north of Australia. Papua New Guinea is one of the most culturally diverse countries in the world. As of 2019, it is also the mostly rural, as only 13.25% of its people live in urban centers. There are 851 known languages in the country, of which 11 now have no known speakers. Most of the population of more than 8 million people live in customary communities, which are as diverse as the languages. The country is one of the world's least explored, culturally and geographically. It is known to have

numerous groups of uncontacted peoples, and researchers believe there are many undiscovered species of plants and animals in the interior.

At the national level, after being ruled by three external powers since 1884, Papua New Guinea established its sovereignty in 1975. This followed nearly sixty years of Australian administration, which started during World War I. It became an independent Commonwealth realm in 1975 with Elizabeth II as its queen. It also became a member of the Commonwealth of Nations in its own right. (Source: Wikipedia)

[3] New Britain is the largest island of the Bismarck Archipelago, in the southwestern Pacific Ocean, in Papua New Guinea. It measures about 370 miles long by 50 miles at its widest, the crescent-shaped island has a 1,000-mile coastline bordered by reefs. (Source: *Encyclopedia Britannica*)

[4] The Missionaries of Charity is a Catholic religious congregation established in 1950 by Mother Teresa, now known in the Catholic Church as Saint Teresa of Calcutta. In 2020, it consisted of 5,167 religious sisters spread throughout the world. (Source: Wikipedia)

CHAPTER 7

Sebastian

————•————

Story from David and Dr. Christa Balch of Sacred Heart
Catholic Church, Salinas, CA

> *Then children were brought to him that He might lay*
> *His hands on them and pray.*

MATTHEW 19:13

D AVID WAS BORN IN A suburb of New York City. His young
life was difficult, since his father left the family when
David was just two years old. His mother remarried
and within eight years his stepfather had a major heart attack
and was unable to go back to work. David's mom had to work
full-time, while she went to school to become a nurse. When
David was fourteen, his stepfather died.

Before his stepfather's death, David was an acolyte in the
Lutheran Church that his family attended on a regular basis.
When his stepfather died, David and his mom stopped attending

church except for Christmas and Easter. When he got to college, he stopped going to church entirely. He went to Columbia University in New York City, and then to Georgetown University in Washington D.C. for law school, graduating *magna cum laude.*

During these years of college and law school, David felt that there was *a void in his life.* Dating, alcohol, and parties did nothing to fill it. He was achieving his goals in school, but something was missing. After law school, he was selected for the prestigious job of law clerk for a federal judge on the US Court of Appeals, Eighth Circuit, which covers seven states. His one-year appointment was in Fargo, North Dakota, which lived up to its reputation for being very cold in the winter.

David was in Fargo to gain special experience and to be able to add another high point on his resume, but *God had other plans that were just beginning to unfold.*

It was to Fargo that Christa went to visit her sister Cathie, who just happened to be working for a judge right next door to where David was working. *They met.* David describes it this way, "I could tell right away that Christa was different—there was a peace about her. She had a sense of who she was, and she was comfortable with herself."

David said, "I could see that she had something that I didn't have, so I asked her what it was. She said that it was Jesus Christ. I sort of laughed at her. She looked at me, smiled, and said, 'I go to church and I have peace; you don't go to church and you don't have peace.'" David sensed that Christa was putting out a challenge with this statement. *It made him think.*

David explained about that first time together, "I knew immediately that I would marry her." The problem was that Christa lived with her parents in Dana Point, California, where she was completing courses in pre-med undergraduate studies, while David still had two months in Fargo working for the Circuit Court judge.

After Christa went back to California, they spoke on the phone for two hours almost every night. Even though this was a distant relationship, they grew closer. On a Fourth of July weekend, David visited Christa in Dana Point. That was the first time they went to church together and David said, "I loved it!"

His job in Fargo ended two months after he met Christa. David was hired by a highly respected law firm in New York City. He found a Catholic parish and signed up for RCIA.[1] Later, when Christa heard about this step, she realized they were headed for marriage. Eleven months later, in 1997, at the Easter Vigil, David became Catholic.

Things really moved quickly from there. Once Christa finished her pre-med studies in California, she applied and was accepted at the School of Medicine at Stoney Brook, sixty miles east of New York City, within a reasonable drive from David.

They married in 1998. When Christa finished medical school, she was accepted for her residency in 2002 at Natividad County

Hospital in Salinas, California, while David was hired as an attorney with a large firm in Salinas.

Christa was soon busy at Natividad Hospital and David at the law firm. They started attending Sacred Heart Church, where Fr. Mike Miller was the pastor. Before he knew it, David found himself in charge of the youth/confirmation group, which included nearly thirty teenagers from the local high schools. It was challenging, but the kids were amazing—David loved them all.

When Christa and David realized that they were not able to have children, they chose to foster infants. After a time in their care, they would adopt the children. That is how Sebastian came into their lives in 2005.

He was special. David described him: "Sebastian was this beautiful little boy, huge smile, long eyelashes—having him in our lives was such a blessing.—He was what you would call 'an old soul.' If he saw somebody on the other side of the playground playing by themselves, he would run over to him and grab his hand and say, 'You come and play with us, come on.'

"Sebastian opened a part of my heart that I thought would be locked forever." David had always held something back of himself from the people, even from Christa. This was perhaps due to his parents' divorce or losing his stepfather early in his life. *David was afraid to be hurt again.*

David said, "With Sebastian it was different." Without words, Sebastian made it clear 'I want all of you.' So, I opened my whole heart to him." It was only a few years later that they adopted Ava.

In 2009, when Sebastian was four-and-a-half, Sebastian and Ava were in Christa's Honda following David home from Salinas about nine p.m. They were separated at the stop light on River Road at the entrance to a housing development. David continued south on the road, while Christa was stuck at the red light.

That is when Christa was rear-ended by a three-ton Dodge pickup truck doing at least fifty-five miles an hour.

When David realized that Christa did not make it home, he traced his path back along River Road, only to discover the tragic accident. The Honda's back half was crushed in. A policeman immediately took him aside and sat him down. David explained to him, "That is my car." The police officer said, "Someone has been hurt in the accident." But a few minutes later, he returned to David and said, "I don't know how to tell you this, but your son was killed in the accident." The officer explained that a drunk driver had not stopped at the red light but plowed into the back of the Honda. All David could say was, "My boy, my boy."

A helicopter soon arrived and took Christa, who was unconscious, and Ava to an emergency hospital in San Jose, which was about sixty miles north. David did not learn the condition of his wife until he arrived at the hospital in San Jose. He was told that she had suffered a head injury, but Ava had minor injuries and would be kept overnight for observation.

At one o'clock in the morning David waited for any news on Christa, who was still unconscious. David explained, "I am someone who has *trust issues*: are people really going to be there, when you need them? *I felt all alone in the world.* And at one o'clock in the morning, Fr. Mike Miller with four of the young adults from the youth group came walking into the hospital, as well as a family from the youth group. They came just to sit with me at one o'clock in the morning an hour drive away.

"For two weeks, I stayed in the hospital, sleeping on the floor, and three of the youth stayed with me. There were these little moments of healing that were taking place…God was saying to me, 'You are not alone in this.' I remember crying as I was driving that first week after the accident, and I said, 'Lord I need a sign that my boy is with you.' I heard this little voice in the back of my head that said, 'Turn on the radio.' So, I turned the radio on. It was *KLOVE*. The words of the first song that came on were: 'I know you are in heaven with the Lord, and I am rejoicing for you, but my heart breaks because I miss you.' Then, two months later I was driving and I said to the Lord, I need a sign that my boy is with you. I heard a little voice that said, 'Turn on the radio' So, I turned on the radio and that same song came on again. And on Sebastian's fifth birthday about six months after the accident, as I drove by the accident site, that song came on again."

For days, Christa was sedated, in-and-out of consciousness. On the third day, David tried to explain to her that Sebastian had died in the accident, but she was unable to understand what he was saying. The funeral was scheduled for ten days after the accident. Later in that first week, David was able to explain that to Christa that Sebastian was dead—they sobbed together. No one else could really understand their pain.

When it came time for David to see Sebastian for the first time in the funeral parlor, God was there to give David strength. David said, "I was outside the room and I knew that he was on the other side, but I couldn't do it. It was almost as if I thought: if I don't walk through that door, this will all be a dream and I will wake up from it.

"Then I said, 'Lord *help me*. I know that I need to do this. I need to see my boy. I need your help.' I literally felt a hand on my shoulder and a peace flooded my soul unlike anything I have ever experienced in my life. And I floated into that room and I held my boy. I sang him songs of Thomas the Tank Engine, Tom and Jerry, and SpongeBob—all the parts he liked.

"In my soul, I was filled up with what I can only describe as the perfect knowledge that Sebastian was alive and he was in heaven. And that I would see him again. I had a feeling of peace that I cannot put into words. At the end of the hour, I walked out back through the door and it all came crashing down on me. It was not as if God had been saying that 'life is going to be great,' but He was saying, 'I am with you. You are not journeying alone, and your boy is safe with me—TRUST ME.'"

On the tenth day, little Sebastian's funeral was held at Sacred Heart's Cislini Center. Christa was still in the hospital, but she could leave to attend the funeral for part of that day. The Cislini Center is a gymnasium, large enough for this special gathering. It was also the place where David had served as director of the Youth Ministry. This tragedy was a difficult day for David and Christa, and it was also a difficult day for the parish, but the healing had begun.

The healing for David and Christa continued even after the funeral.

David led a retreat one night at the Mission San Antonio De Padua seventy miles south of Salinas for a group of teenagers. This is how David described his experience, "I started sharing my stories about Sebastian. At the end of my sharing stories about my son, a boy came up to me and said, 'David, I'm sorry, I really couldn't pay attention to what you were saying because all I could hear was the sound of a little boy running around this church in joyful laughter.' All I could do was smile."

Christa recounted this story to me, "One night several months after coming home from the hospital, I had a particularly sad and mad night. I was up a lot and prayed in a most desperate way. I told God that I just needed to know that Sebastian was okay.

"The next day, I was in the grocery store. Around the corner of the aisle that I was in, came a girl from my husband's youth/confirmation group. When she saw me, she gasped and put her hand to her mouth and backed out of the aisle.

"I wasn't sure what to think.

"Soon, she came back around the corner with her mother and sister surrounding her. They explained that she had been up since three a.m., having trouble trying to process things. She had been awakened by my Sebastian at that time. She knew Sebastian well because my husband had brought him to the youth group often. Sebastian appeared to her, smiling and at peace. She asked him, if he could come back, would he? She said he got a look in his eyes that expressed how wonderful heaven was, and said, 'No, but tell my mom I miss her.'

"God gave me what I needed at the time—to know that Sebastian was better than okay; that he was in a better place with the Lord; he was happy; that he was aware of me on some level, and that he loved me.

"This revelation got me through the following years with a peace and grace that may not have been possible otherwise."

PRAISE GOD!

NOTE: Ava only had minor injuries because of the accident and is now a healthy teenager.

Christa and David have adopted three infants in addition to Ava.

David led the youth/confirmation group for a total of thirteen years before redirecting that time to his growing family.

David is a full-time attorney and Christa is a doctor in a private practice.

At the trial, David and Christa stood up in court and forgave the drunk driver, and years later worked to reduce his sentence to nine years from the sixteen that he had been sentenced. David explained, "Forgiving the driver was a key part of our own healing."

———•———

[1] **RCIA** (The Rite of Christian Initiation of Adults) is a process developed by the Catholic Church for prospective converts to Catholicism who are above the age of infant baptism. Candidates are introduced to aspects of Catholic beliefs and practices over a six-month or longer period of weekly small-group meetings with other interested prospective converts, as well as members of the parish who act as sponsors. Guest speakers are often local priests or the pastor of the parish. During this period, close friendships are built that provide a sense of community and welcoming, as well as period of openness to learn about the Catholic Church.

CHAPTER 8

Trust in God

———•———

Story from Rev. Michael Miller of St. Margaret Mary Catholic Church, Chino, California

Trust in the Lord with all your heart,
on your own intelligence rely not;
In all your ways be mindful of him,
and he will make straight your paths.

PROVERBS 3:5, 6

HIS LIPS WERE MOVING, AND sound was coming out, but it might as well be without sound because Fr. Mike could not understand a word that Fr. Juan was saying. Spanish was not a language that Fr. Mike understood. But it was clear that what Fr. Juan was saying to the congregation *was bad.* Fr. Mike might not be able to read lips or understand Spanish, but he could read the expression on the parishioners' faces.

This was not a good way to begin his first pastoral position.

After Mass was over, Fr. Mike learned from some parishioners that Fr. Juan said that the church, the old Sacred Heart Church in Hollister, was ugly and a fire hazard and should be torn town. He said that they should build a new church.

The people loved that old church. This was the church where they had made their first communion, baptized their children, and were married. They did not like what Fr. Juan had said about their church, because it was like their own home to them.

Fr. Mike soon realized that Fr. Juan himself was very upset. It all had gone back to an anointing that he had performed weeks earlier on the victims of a terrible fire, which left the victims unrecognizable. Fr. Juan had been so traumatized that he must have seen Sacred Heart Church as another fire hazard and imagined another tragedy.

With all of these thoughts and problems going through Fr. Mike's mind, he still had to perform his role of priest. On Monday morning, he returned to the sanctuary to celebrate the Spanish daily Mass. There were thirty to forty parishioners present.

Fr. Mike learned right before Mass that the assigned reader had not shown up, so when it came to the time for the first reading, Fr. Mike asked in his very broken Spanish, "Would someone please come up and do the reading?"

There was a long pause that soon became a very *uncomfortable pause*. Fr. Mike said, "I started to get more nervous and more mad and more mad and more nervous, and finally a young man named Mauricio stood up and came forward. He bowed before the altar and then walked to the ambo and stood there. And then he was quiet.

"I couldn't be mad at him, since he was trying to help, but I did think, 'What is going on?' So I went over to him and whispered, 'Mauricio, what is going on?' He said, 'I can't read!'"

Fr. Mike continued, "Mauricio thought that if no one else would go up to read that he had to try, trusting in God to help him. He stood there risking all that embarrassment and humiliation. The people saw this and understood what was happening. They were so touched that three of them came forward to read for him.

"I never had a problem again finding readers at daily Mass. God didn't give me one reader, but three because Mauricio was humble enough to obey God."

PRAISE GOD!

NOTE: Fr. Mike Miller has been the pastor at St. Margaret Mary's Catholic Church for the last eight years and is planning to retire in June to work with the homeless.

His story, *"The Hitchhiker"* is Chapter 3 in *GOD Incidents— True Stories of God Working in the Lives of Catholics (Book I)*. *It is one of the author's all-time favorite stories and it was the first one written.*

CHAPTER 9

Hope Restored

———•———

Story from Josie Bagtas of Sacred Heart Church, Salinas, California

And hope does not disappoint, because the love of God
has been poured out into our hearts through
the Holy Spirit that has been given to us.

ROMANS 5:5

JOSIE WAS BORN IN THE Philippines. She was one of nine children in her family. When she was twenty-five, she went to Chicago to work in a nursing home for the elderly. She was one of five nurses that arrived together from the Philippines.

While working in Chicago, she met Virgil. They married and had two boys, Anthony and Lloyd. Later, they moved to Salinas, where Josie worked at Salinas Memorial Hospital as the head nurse in the Critical Care ward. It was there that she suffered an injury to her upper back while moving an overweight patient from a gurney to his bed. Before they were able to diagnose the extent of her injury, she was in a car accident where she was rear-ended, causing even more damage to her back. X-rays revealed a severe spinal injury that required fusion of her C-2 through C-6 discs. After eight months of recovery, she returned to work at reduced hours, trying to work up to a full day.

Within a year, Josie found herself unemployed. She presented too much of a liability to the hospital. Given the seriousness of her surgery, the hospital felt she could be paralyzed at any time. If this were not enough burden, Virgil lost his job when his company moved back East. Now they were both unemployed.

"God is faithful and will not let you be tried beyond your strength; but with the trial he will also provide a way out, so that you may be able to bear it." 1 Corinthians 10:13

Josie began attending daily Mass and Friday adoration.[1] Since she was there every day, she soon took over the role of sacristan[2]— setting up the altar for the 12:15 Mass. She also was a lector and extraordinary minister of Holy Communion. During this time, her source of strength was the Eucharist, and adoration in front of the tabernacle after Mass. *Jesus was her only hope.*

On one day, when Josie was especially down on her life's trials, she found herself on her knees sobbing in front of the tabernacle. She called out to God for help. In a special moment of clarity, Josie heard God in that *soft inner voice* say, "Serve me and I will never abandon or forsake you." Her sobbing stopped immediately—she now had hope to move forward with her life.

After that event, things started to fall in place. Virgil was again employed. Lloyd was accepted at UC Irvine and was selected over many other applicants to work in the university bookstore. This helped with college expenses. Anthony received a scholarship to finish Palma High School and was hired to play piano at the Saturday evening Mass at St. Joseph's Catholic Church in Spreckels. Then, three other parishes hired him as well. He saved this money for college.

Josie's overall feelings became more positive, because she knew God had promised: "Serve me and I will never abandon or forsake you."

At this time, many young people were being killed by gang violence in Salinas. So, Josie and a parish friend, Catherine O'Brien, approached their pastor, Fr. Mike Miller, to start a Eucharistic procession every *first Friday* of the month. This would require a priest or deacon to carry the monstrance[3] around the half-mile procession, while a group of parishioners followed along praying the rosary for an end to the gang violence. Fr. Mike agreed to their proposal and often took part in the monthly Eucharistic procession.

On one particular first Friday, Deacon Rick Gutierrez led the procession, carrying the Blessed Sacrament in the monstrance. The procession was to begin and end at the altar in the church. However, during the procession another parish group was in the church practicing for an event on the following day. When the procession returned to church, Deacon Rick carried the monstrance into the adjacent parish office and set the monstrance on a table. Josie and the others remained with the Blessed Sacrament, finishing up the rosary while Deacon Rick went into the church.

Josie knelt before the Blessed Sacrament and prayed with her head down. When she looked up at the exposed Host, she saw instead the image of Jesus crowned with thorns, bleeding. She thought that she must be imagining it, so she closed her eyes, but when she opened them again, the image remained. This brought tears of sorrow mixed with joy, for Jesus had revealed His image to her. She could only thank God for sharing this vision with her. PRAISE GOD!

NOTE: Josie continues to serve God as a sacristan and as a sponsor for the RCIA program that begins in the fall and continues to the Easer Vigil Mass.

---

[1] **Adoration:** The Catechism of the Catholic Church states, "Adoration is the acknowledgement of God as God, creator and savior, the Lord and master of everything that exists as infinite and merciful love" (CCC #2096). "Adoration is homage of the spirit to the King of glory, respectful silence in the presence of the ever-greater God" (CCC #2628).

[2] A **sacristan** is a person appointed for the care of the sacristy, sacred vessels, vestments, and other articles required by the ceremonial for any liturgical function. (Source: Catholicculture.org)

[3] A **monstrance** is a metal vessel usually gold- or silver-plated with a transparent section in which the Sacred Host is placed in its lunette when exposed for Adoration or carried in procession. It varies in shape and ornamentation, popular models being tower-shaped or round, and a metal circlet surrounded with rays or bars resting on a stem rising from a heavy base, many ornamented with jewels. (Source: The Catholic Dictionary)

CHAPTER 10

Mary's Veil

—◦—

Story from Daniela Desiderio of Mission San Juan Bautista in San Juan Bautista, California

Remember, oh most gracious Virgin Mary,
that never was it known that anyone who fled to thy protection,
implored thy help, or sought thy intersession was left unaided.
Inspired by this confidence, I fly unto thee,
O Virgin of virgins, my mother; to thee do I come,
before thee I stand, sinful and sorrowful.
O Mother of the Word Incarnate, despise not my petitions,
but in thy mercy hear and answer me.
Amen.

MEMORARE PRAYER

WHEN DANIELA WAS NINETEEN YEARS old and living in California, she realized that she had not seen her sister, Irene, in several years; so, when she had enough vacation time accumulated, she flew to Mexico City with plans to spend a month with her sister and visit with family and old friends. *She had no idea how memorable this time would be when she stepped off the plane.*

Her adventure all started with a trip with her two friends, Monica and Tony, across the city in the bus and then the metro to an event at her nephew's private school. By the time it was over, it was late in the day and they felt an urgency to start home. *It was getting dark.*

The metro ride was the longest part of their trip. By the time they left the metro to find a bus for the final leg of the trip, *it was dark.* Because the regular bus was full, they were forced to take a smaller minibus.

When they stopped at the train station, three young men got on the bus. One walked to the back, one stood in the middle, and the third stood at the front. Daniela said, "I didn't like the way they looked. I was worried." About that time, the young man in the front of the bus pulled out a gun from under his coat and demanded that the passengers give them not just their money, but anything of value, including clothes and shoes.

Daniela was sitting next to the window, terrified. She began to shake in fear. One of the men grabbed Monica and demanded that she give him her purse and threatened to kill her. As the robbers moved within the minibus making threats and demands of the passengers, Daniella prayed to the Virgin Mary as her mom had taught her. "Virgin Mary, Virgin Mary, cover me with your veil, so that they will not see me. Please cover me; please cover me with your veil."

The robber stopped at Tony next and took his wallet and demanded that he give them his jacket. Daniela knew that she was next, so she sat in silence, shaking, looking down, but he passed right by her.

Everyone on the bus was robbed that day, except Daniela. PRAISE GOD!!

NOTE: Daniela works in the Mission of San Juan Bautista parish office as a secretary, but she will never forget that day on the minibus in Mexico City.

CHAPTER 11

Here I am, Lord

Story from Kevin Czarnecki of Our Lady of the Woods Catholic Church, Orland Park, Illinois

Go to sleep and if you are called reply,
"Speak Lord for your servant is listening."

1 SAMUEL 3:9

K EVIN WAS BORN TO DAN and Marianne Czarnecki. He was the third child of four: Pete was the oldest, followed by Katherine, then Kevin, and finally Michelle. His father, Dan, was a firefighter working two twenty-four-hour day shifts, with a day off in between. In addition, he had a variety of other jobs during the week to support his family. Marianne had the ideal job for a mom because her work hours coincided with the children's school hours.

His parent's commitment to the Church could be seen in the importance they placed by sending their children to Catholic grammar school through high school. On Sundays, they all attended Mass as a family. *It was the influence of his family's life that would later play a part in Kevin's life decisions.*

As an altar boy, Kevin not only learned to love the Mass, but also gained an insight into the life of the priests—he learned that they were just men doing a special role in the service of God. He liked the priests whom he assisted at Mass. "I got to know the priests very well. I grew up with the sense that these were just men doing a wonderful thing in serving God in this way. They were accessible to me and I loved being an attendant to them at the altar."

Kevin went to an all-boy high school. In his junior year, he attended a Kairos[1] retreat which is a three-day weekend that was put on by a group of seniors who had attended the Kairos retreat the previous year. A priest was also part of the team.

Kevin learned that the purpose of Kairos was to introduce the students to Jesus Christ in a deeper way, to call them into mature discipleship, and to walk with them as they responded. Kairos had a huge impact on Kevin, so much so that he chose to return the following year as a team member and presenter.

This experience was the first step in which God had touched Kevin in a significant way. At that time, he even considered priesthood, but when he mentioned this to his football coach, the coach dismissed the idea with a laugh.

"I was just a high school kid trying to find my way in life."

After graduation, Kevin attended St. Norbert College near Green Bay, Wisconsin. His overall plan was to teach high school. He continued attending Mass every weekend, now on his own.

It was at St. Norbert College in his sophomore year that he again thought of going into the priesthood. He decided to visit St. Joseph's Seminary and learn what he would have to do to make this happen. He learned that he could easily transfer to the seminary, especially since he was already a philosophy minor. When he returned to his college, he mentioned these thoughts of priesthood to his friends, but again they dismissed the idea. *It seemed that no one could relate to becoming a priest, so no one would say a word of encouragement to him. Instead, he decided to wait for more direction from God.*

After graduation, Kevin felt that he needed some time before going into a master's program for his teaching certificate. "I wanted to do something … I wanted to figure out where I was supposed to fit in the world." So, he spent one year of service with AmeriCorps[2] on the East Coast. "It was a good experience. It consisted of building houses, and later, working in a national park." He discovered that in the AmeriCorps, the only way he could get to church was to hitch a ride with the government-sanctioned van and time it just right to get a ride back with them when Mass was over. Kevin realized that he had taken Mass for granted—it was only when it was going to be denied to him that he felt the real true value of it.

After the year in AmeriCorps, he worked in Denver with the Colorado Vincentian Volunteers, teaching at Annunciation

Catholic School with the Sisters of Charity. The following year, he found a path to get his teaching certification through Regis University and the Diocese of Denver by teaching fourth grade at Guardian Angels Catholic School in northwest Denver. It was while working there that Kevin developed a regular prayer life combined with reading Scripture.

Everything was going wonderfully until his great-uncle died in January 2006. *His great-uncle had been like the grandfather that he had never had.*

He returned home to Orland Park, Illinois, for the funeral. The family gathered for the funeral Mass, which was celebrated by his uncle, Fr. Michael Foley. It was a beautiful service. It was especially meaningful because he was back with his family, and it gave him a chance to speak with Fr. Mike. There was nothing special that was said about his call to the priesthood, but because of this conversation, Kevin again felt the tug to become a priest. Perhaps it was just the influence of seeing a family member celebrating Mass.

This time, he decided to respond to the call: "Here I am Lord; I come to do your will." So, in May, at the end of his teaching year, he enrolled in Mundelein Seminary at the University of Saint Mary of the Lake and began studies in August 2006. He was placed in a pre-theology curriculum, where he studied philosophy, language, and the Bible. The highlight of his classes was philosophy, which was taught by Fr. Robert Barron (now Bishop Barron). Although he was learning a lot, and he had also developed a wonderful prayer life, there was something missing. Kevin explained it this way, "I felt like an imposter, like I didn't belong there."

In the seminary chapel of the Immaculate Conception, on the wall behind the altar, was a beautiful painting of God the Father, who was portrayed as an elderly figure set in the clouds. The Holy Spirit was depicted as a dove below Him, and the Blessed Mother was at the bottom of the painting holding the right hand of Jesus, pictured as a young boy of about ten.

Jesus was holding a staff in His left hand, while next to Him was the figure of St. Joseph with his right arm extended toward Jesus but not touching Him. The fact that St. Joseph was not portrayed holding Jesus's hand seemed wrong to Kevin. This conflict that he saw in the painting reflected Kevin's sense of his life there at the seminary. "It didn't feel complete." He saw himself like St. Joseph, as not belonging … *an outsider.*

It all came to a head at the *March for Life* on January 22, 2007. Kevin was part of the vigil Mass at the Basilica of the National Shrine of the Immaculate Conception in Washington, DC. He was one of hundreds of seminarians who processed into a standing-room-only basilica. It was not the size of the basilica, or the number of people that got to Kevin. It was the many mothers and fathers holding their children to help them see the procession of seminarians, deacons, priests, and bishops. Kevin said, "These fathers and mothers were testifying to the beauty that is family life. I felt that I should not be in the procession, but in the pew myself with a family.

"At that time, I knew in good conscience that I must leave the seminary. At the request of my spiritual director, I remained through the semester, but on May 16, 2007, after bearing witness to the ordination of that year's graduating class and serving as emcee at a confirmation later that same day, I returned my cassock and headed toward my future with an open heart.

"I knew that while my time in the seminary was a blessing, since it opened up an interior prayer life as I had never imagined before—I was drawn toward a different vocation—that of a married high school teacher back in my hometown of Orland Park."

NOTE: Kevin's story continues in the following chapter.

[1] **Kairos** (from Greek καιρός,") is a Roman Catholic retreat program for high school and college. Kairos is part of the larger three-day movement in America, ultimately derived from the Cursillo movement founded in Majorca, Spain, in 1944. (Source: Wikipedia)

[2] **AmeriCorps** is a voluntary civil society program supported by the US federal government, foundations, corporations, and other donors that engages adults in public service work with a goal of "helping others and meeting critical needs in the community." (Source: Wikipedia)

CHAPTER 12

Letting Go

—————•————

Story from Christine Czarnecki of Our Lady of the Woods
Catholic Church, Orland Park, Illinois

*We know that all things work for good for those who love God,
who are called according to His purpose.*

ROMANS 8:28

*This is part of Kevin's story continued
from the previous chapter.*

CHRISTINE WAS BORN TO JIM and Judy Motola. However, when Christine was two years old, her parents divorced. Even though they were divorced, they remained on friendly terms. Jim stayed in Christine's life and financially supported her Catholic education through high school. Christine never heard harsh words between her parents. Jim still cared for Judy, and he tried his best to be a loving father to Christine.

Christine's mom had a strong Catholic faith that she did her best to share with her daughter. She taught Christine how important God should be in her life. Christine and her mom always went to church together, and in high school, Judy took her daughter to a Bible study group of Christian friends. This experience led Christine to become an even stronger Catholic because now she could see the basis of her faith in Scripture, and her love for Jesus increased.

When she went off to the University of Illinois in Chicago, she stopped attending church, but God remained in her life. It was while she was in college at the age of twenty that she met Mike. They began dating.

At that age, emotion often leads one in decision-making, while God is then pushed into the background.

Christine's friends were getting married while she and Mike continued to date. Time was slipping away. Christine graduated from the university and began teaching at the elementary school. Between teaching and dating, Christine saw more friends not only marry but have children, while she and Mike continued to date. Their relationship did not seem to be going anywhere. After eight and a half years of dating, in a response to an argument, Mike proposed. Finally, it had come to talk of marriage, their marriage.

Over the next year and a half, marriage arrangements were made. Bridesmaids were chosen and the hall for the reception was booked. But with all the planning, *Christine started to have doubts.* It came to a head one night when she lay in bed emotionally upset, but she wasn't sure why. So much was being planned for the wedding, but *something wasn't right.* Wide awake and restless, unable to sleep, out of her mouth came these words, "Goodbye, Mike." Suddenly, a peace came over her. *It was as if God were telling her that it was over … This is not what He had planned for her.*

Later, she unloaded all her concerns with a close friend, who said, "It sounds like you know what you have to do. You just need to do it." That was easy for her friend to say, but it was much more complicated to actually do.

When she expressed her concerns to Mike, they tried counseling, but afterward all Mike could say was, "I don't think I can give you what you want." Christine's response was, "What is it that you can't give me?"

It now was clear that their ten years of building a relationship and making plans for marriage had come to an end. It was only four months before the planned wedding. Fortunately, they had not sent out any invitations.

Christine had let ten years of her life slip away. Now she faced dealing with the deep pain of that failed relationship. Over the next months, friends arranged for her to date guys they knew, but it only added to the questions that filled her mind that focused on what had gone wrong—what she could have done differently, etc. She really wasn't ready for another serious relationship.

It all came to a head one day in church. She couldn't focus on the Mass or the homily because her mind was focused instead on her failed relationship and the frustration of what should she do next.

"I remember thinking, 'I'm done.' I could see my past life spinning in front of my face. I tried to grab it, but I could not control it. I could not hold on to it. I told God, 'I'm done. I don't know what to do and I don't know what you want. I don't know what I'm supposed to be doing. My life is yours. I'm done!'"

At that point, Christine heard an audible voice from God say, "Thank you, now that you are out of my way, I can do what I need to do." Christine recalls a peace came over her and she felt a lifting of her control over everything. *It was as if God had taken control and she was at peace with it.*

It was not as if everything had changed, but Christine now felt that she should just live her life and let God do what He promised. She only wondered what it was that God was going to do. What was it that "God needed to do?"

Six months after breaking up with Mike, Christine was having dinner with Vicki, her student teacher roommate, when Vicki received a text from her former boyfriend, Jeremy. He gave her the phone number of his best friend, Kevin, because he thought Christine might like to meet him.

Two days later, they actually met. Christine described it this way: "I remember that our first meeting was the most comfortable conversation that I had ever had." Kevin had a wonderful voice that Christine immediately liked. Christine learned that Kevin taught in the local Catholic high school, and he had even been in the seminary before that. His uncle was the pastor of a nearby Catholic church.

The first date was followed by others and by the end of the first week Christine said, "I knew that I would marry him." The next week, Christine and her mom had to go to a wake and Kevin wanted to come. He said, "I like going to wakes and praying for people." That left a lasting impression on Christine and her mom.

By May, they were already talking about getting married. They made arrangements to meet with a priest to discuss the sacrament of marriage. Christine said, "Kevin started acting funny, as we walked around the outside of the parish grounds. Then, suddenly, he went down on one knee and proposed."

God had kept His promise, and Christine was delighted that *God had chosen Kevin for her spouse.*

NOTE: Christine and Kevin were married December 6, 2008. They have three boys: Cohen 7, Camden 9, and Carter 11.

CHAPTER 13

Birthday Surprise

———•———

Story from Tom Lukes of Our Lady of Mt. Carmel in Carmel Valley, California

Whoever eats my flesh and drinks my blood has eternal life and I will raise him up on the last day.

JOHN 6:54

I HAD JUST STEPPED INTO THE shower long enough to wet my hair when it hit me. In two weeks, on April 14th, I would be turning sixty. A slight shiver went through me—a sense of dread. I thought when I turned fifty, nothing like this bothered me. Why now?

I remember that when I was in my twenties, I thought that I would not make it to thirty, but obviously that was wrong. This was different—it was more of a dread. I completed my shower without any more thoughts on this upcoming birthday and soon was headed to morning Mass at Sacred Heart Church.

Well, as it turned out, that morning shower experience was not repeated, and in fact, I never thought about my birthday again.

In the early morning of my birthday, as I slept, I had the most wonderful dream. I was at Sacred Heart Church. I was in front of the tabernacle. I opened the door of the tabernacle and genuflected, like I always did. I reached in and removed the ciborium.[1] I held it with both hands wrapped around the curved portion of the cup with reverence. At that moment, I was enveloped by a wonderful hug from my Savior. It was as real, as if it really happened.

I awoke, with the thought: *This is a great way to be greeted on my sixtieth birthday.*

PRAISE GOD!

———◆◆———

[1] **Ciborium** in the Catholic Church is any receptacle designed to hold the consecrated Eucharist of the Catholic Church. The ciborium is usually shaped like a rounded goblet, or chalice, with a dome-shaped cover. (Source: Britannica.com)

CHAPTER 14

Love Is Kind

—•—

Story from Patti Stluka of Our Lady of the Woods in Orland Park, Illinois

Whatever you ask for in prayer with faith you will receive.

MATTHEW 21:22

IT ALL STARTED WITH A simple wave to a stranger, as Patti drove down to her new home with her husband. The wave reflected Patti's loving character and upbringing. Patti had always been a naturally friendly girl.

Raised in the city of Chicago, she was the second oldest of four children in the family. Debbie was the oldest, followed by Patti, then Kathy, and finally Tom. "Our faith was a very big part of our family life. We not only went to Mass every Sunday, but we went every day during Lent." Getting to Mass involved a mile and a half walk each way. This was just part of the Lenten sacrifice.

When Patti was thirteen, the family was devastated by the death of their father. Patti's "stay-at-home" mom was forced to find a job and the four kids were challenged to contribute as much as possible to help their mom to keep up the house and take care of each other. Food stamps helped, and none of the kids every asked their mom about going on vacation. They all knew that was no longer possible, but none of the kids complained.

The chores assigned in the past had to be expanded to help their mom deal with the crisis. As Patti explained it, "The chores became *acts of love*—we all knew that mom needed all the help she could get for us to survive as a family."

After their father died, Patti's mom had their priest come to the house and have the Sacred Heart[1] "enthroned" in their house. Patti said, "Every night we would gather around the dining room table and say the prayer to the Sacred Heart."

> *Come Lord Jesus, humbly kneeling at Your feet, we renew the consecration of our family to Your Divine Heart. Be our King forever. In You we have full and entire confidence. May Your spirit penetrate our thoughts, our desires, our words, and our deeds. Bless our undertakings; share in our joys, in our trials and in our labors. Grant us to know You better, to love You more, and to serve you without faltering.*
>
> *By the Immaculate Heart of Mary, Queen of Peace, set up Your kingdom in our country. Enter closely into the midst of our families and make them Your own through*

the solemn enthronement of Your Sacred Heart. So that soon one cry may resound from home to home. May the triumphant Heart of Jesus be everywhere loved, blessed, and glorified forever. Honor and glory to the Sacred Heart of Jesus and Mary. Sacred Heart of Jesus protect our families." Amen. (Source: Patti Stluka)

Both Patti and Debbie had jobs that helped contribute to the family's expenses. In fact, Patti was hired the year her dad died at a fast-food restaurant at the age of thirteen. Since by law, you had to be sixteen to work, the manager simply edited her birth certificate. By the end of the year, she was elevated to "closing store manager." Working that young helped her to understand responsibility and it gave her a strong work ethic. Pattie said, "You learn how to work hard." Debbie and Patti were just helping Mom pay the bills, but in doing so they were learning much more.

As time went by, the family continued their devotion to the Sacred Heart and continued to attend Sunday Mass. This strong foundation helped Mom deal with the typical problems of a family with four kids and no father. *It was in their faith that they were strong.*

As time went by, the kids grew old enough to move out of the home and raise their own families. Patti married and moved to Orland Park, a suburb of Chicago. The stranger down the street to whom she had waved became her closest friend.

Her name was Vickie Carlo.

Vickie attended St. Francis Catholic Church nearby, while Patti and her husband, Keith, attended Our Lady of the Woods. But attending different Catholic churches did not affect their friendship.

Both had their first child about the same time, so all the concerns of bearing and later caring for their first child helped them grow even closer. Then came their second pregnancy, and again they had the same experience. It was not planned, but God seemed to be helping these young mothers not only share the joys of motherhood, but also have a friend in the same situation. This was a wonderful way to deepen Patti and Vickie's friendship. Then, as the children grew older, the two families did everything together—the children naturally became very close too, since they were the same age and grew up together.

When Patti's oldest child was four, her husband, Keith, announced he wanted a divorce and left her. Patti realized that she, like her mom, had to raise a family without a father in the house.

Vickie's family shared in Patti's grief. They too felt the pain as if one of their family members had died. Vickie would come over and be a "sounding board" for Patti day and night. Just having someone who was willing to comfort her made a big difference in helping Patti deal with her deep hurt. *"Love is kind..." (1 Corinthians 13: 4).*

On July 26ᵗʰ, Vickie attended Mass at her mom's church, St. Anne's Catholic Church, to celebrate the feast of St. Anne. Everyone in attendance received a holy card with a novena prayer to St. Anne. Vickie gave the card to Patti in hopes that it would be a prayer to a saint that would help and comfort her. (St. Anne is Blessed Virgin Mary's own mother.)

Novena Prayer to St. Anne

Glorious St. Anne, filled with compassion for those who invoke you, and with love for those who suffer, heavily laden with the weight of my troubles, I cast myself at your feet and humbly beg of you to take the present affair which I recommend to you under special protection.

I beg you to recommend it to your daughter, the Blessed Virgin Mary, and lay it before the throne of Jesus, so that He may bring it to a happy issue. Cease not to intercede for me until the request is granted. Above all, obtain for me the grace of one day beholding my God face to face, and with you and Mary and all the saints, praising and blessing Him to all eternity.

Good St. Anne, mother of her who is our Life our Sweetness and our Hope, pray to her for us, and obtain our request. Amen.

Patti found comfort in the prayer and used it often during her time after Keith left her and the two kids. The prayer was very helpful, but eventually the card went in the drawer and was soon forgotten. After that experience, Pattie's prayers returned directly to God and to God and Mary through the rosary.

It was years later, when Patti's oldest sister, Debbie, was hospitalized for cancer treatment that Patti came across St. Anne's prayer card in her drawer. She thought that she would pray the novena to St. Anne for help for her sister. She asked St. Anne, "Be with my sister, to give her strength, to give her peace, and to help her family." For nine days Patti said the novena prayer to St. Anne, and then she would start a new novena.

Daily, Patti went to see her sister at the hospital, but she said, one day, "I felt that I needed a long walk. I decided to say the novena prayer as I was walking. I still remember that as I was in the middle of the prayer when this other prayer came to mind. 'Love is patient, love is kind . . .' and I thought that this described my sister, Debbie. It was comforting to have this second prayer remind me of the kind of person my sister was. I then went back to the novena and finished up the prayer.

"Later that afternoon, a group of us gathered in Debbie's hospital room to pray and just be with Debbie. One of Debbie's friends from her parish led a prayer for her. He started by saying that although this was not a typical prayer for times like this, he was moved to repeat this Bible verse 'Love is Patient, Love is Kind, It Does Not Envy . . .'" Patti thought that "it was an amazing coincidence"—she had the same prayer pop in her mind earlier.

A day or two later Debbie passed away.

"It was not until a couple of months later that I went to put that novena card back in a drawer and happened to notice for the first time St. Anne's Feast Day was July 26th." Debbie died on St. Anne's feast day! *Another God incident!*

"Love is patient, love is kind . . ." (1 Corinthians 13:4)

NOTE: Sometimes love is manifested through friends like Vickie— just when we need to be loved—and sometimes God helps us see the qualities of love in those we care for. We must recognize these special moments and cherish them.

---

[1] **Sacred Heart of Jesus.** The Solemnity of the Sacred Heart is celebrated throughout the world on the Friday following the Feast of Corpus Christi. Every year, nineteen days after Pentecost, the Catholic Church celebrates the Solemnity of the Sacred Heart of Jesus. Devotion to the wounded heart of Jesus has its origins in the eleventh century, when pious Christians meditated on the Five Wounds of Christ. There grew up among the faithful prayers to the Sacred Heart, prayers to the Shoulder Wound of Christ—private devotions that helped Christians to focus on the Passion and Death of Christ, and thus to grow in love for our Savior who had suffered and died for us. It was not until 1670, however, that a French priest, Fr. Jean Eudes, celebrated the first Feast of the Sacred Heart. Around the same time, a pious sister, Margaret Mary Alacoque, began to report visions of Jesus. He appeared to her frequently, and in December 1673 he permitted Margaret Mary to rest her head upon His Heart. As she experienced the comfort of His Presence, Jesus told her of His great love and explained that He had chosen her to make His love and His goodness known to all. The following year, in June or July of 1674, Margaret Mary reported that Jesus wanted to be honored under the figure of His Heart of flesh. He asked the faithful to receive Him in the Eucharist frequently, especially on the First Friday of the month, and to observe a Holy Hour of devotion to Him.

In 1675, during the octave of Corpus Christi, Margaret Mary received the vision which came to be known as the "great apparition." Jesus asked that the modern Feast of the Sacred Heart be celebrated each year on the Friday following Corpus Christi, in reparation for the ingratitude of men for the sacrifice that Christ had made for them.

CHAPTER 15

My Little Angels

---•---

Story from Barbara Cesarec of Lumen Christi Catholic Church in Mequon, WI

Have no anxiety at all, but in everything, by prayer and petition,
with thanksgiving, make your request known to God.
Then the peace of God that surpasses all understanding
will guard your hearts and minds in Christ Jesus.

PHILIPPIANS 4:6–7

BARBARA WAS THE OLDEST GIRL of four children. Her mom and dad had both graduated from Marquette University, when it was uncommon for a woman to even go to college. All the children attended Catholic grammar school and high school. They lived a typical Catholic life in the 1950s and 1960s.

The family's treatment of Holy Week offers insight into this holy family.

On Good Friday, Barbara and her siblings spent the noon hour through 3 pm in their bedrooms silently reflecting on Christ's death on the cross and His holy sacrifice for mankind. This practice also kept the house unusually quiet, which allowed the parents a special time of reflection and peace.

On Easter Sunday, they all went to church to celebrate Jesus's Resurrection. It was amazing how often Easter Sunday weather was sunny and beautiful, almost as if God wanted that day to be special, whereas Good Friday was often dark and raining—*tears from heaven*—to reflect Jesus's suffering on that day. On Easter Sunday, Barbara's mom always wore her Easter hat, and the kids dressed up in their Sunday best. That was a typical Easter for the Cesarec family.

Barbara always wanted to be an airline stewardess, but her dad encouraged her to first go to college. He said, "Take care of your education first, and then you can decide about being an airline stewardess." She is always grateful that she followed his advice.

God helped her find her calling—one that would bring her happiness. Here's how that came about. While in high school, she said, "I babysat for every kid on the block, but I didn't sit around and drink Coke and watch TV." Instead, she made that time together fun for the kids. She said, "We would play games. We would pretend we were pilots and jump off chairs. One day, I realized *I loved children*." So, Barbara decided to major in elementary education and she eventually received a master's degree in reading.

After graduation, Barbara worked as a teacher in inner city Milwaukee until a series of events convinced her to leave. First, her car was stolen; then, while she was eating lunch in the teacher's lounge, she was accosted by a stranger. She said, "I still remember that day. I asked the stranger if he were a parent, and for the name of his child's teacher. When he couldn't supply the name of the teacher, I ran toward the school office for assistance. Fortunately, the man fled the building." The final event was when a local public schoolteacher was placed in her own car trunk while her home was robbed. If someone had not heard her screaming, she might have died from suffocation.

It was time to move to the suburbs.

As a kindergarten teacher, Barbara had a unique way of preparing the children for their first experience with school. She would call their home and say, "Hello, this is Mrs. Cesarec, Johnny's teacher. Can I speak with him?" She would then tell Johnny that she was his teacher, and they were going to have a lot of fun at school. She would ask him things like, "What color is your backpack? What is your favorite game?" This early contact with the kids allowed her to take away the fear of their first day at school. One excited kindergartener said to his mom, "My teacher says were going to have fun at school."

Barbara really loved her students: "They are my little angels."

In her mid-fifties, after teaching for more than twenty years, Barbara discovered that she was having trouble hearing. She first noticed it when she used the phone—it was only her right ear that was the problem. When she switched to her left ear, she could hear fine. She thought it was just a temporary thing, but after weeks, it did not improve.

Being married to a physician proved helpful, so she asked her husband, Bob, to bring his otoscope[1] home to check out her ear. That night, Bob couldn't see anything wrong, but he suggested she have an exam by an ENT (ears, nose, and throat) doctor.

Thus, began a series of doctor visits. The ENT doctor identified a small bone pressing against the ear drum, distorting it but probably not affecting Barbara's hearing. The specialist suggested an MRI to look for a possible tumor in the inner ear.

The radiologist who was to perform the MRI was also a friend of her husband, so he asked Bob if he would like to witness the MRI. Bob agreed. As Barbara listened to the hammering that is a normal part of the MRI process, Bob and the radiologist were in the control room witnessing the image of not only Barbara's ear, but also part of her cheek and eye that the MRI also captured.

They noticed a large mass under her cheek that extended under her eye. Bob knew immediately that it was a tumor, but he had no way of knowing whether it was cancerous or not. The room became very silent and all the radiologist could say was, "Oh!" Afterward, neither said anything to Barbara about what they had seen; even on the drive home with Barbara, Bob said nothing.

Barbara said, "I'll never forget that night." After dinner, Bob told her what the MRI had revealed. He said that they would need to go to the cancer institute in Milwaukee right away to see a cancer specialist.

What had started with a hearing problem in her right ear had turned into a *nightmare*. All she could think about were her little angels. The question in her mind was, "On that most important first day of school, will I be greeting them with a warm smile, or will they meet a substitute teacher?"

The next morning, they drove to the Froedtert Medical Center *in silence*. The visit to see the specialist had both Barbara and Bob on edge, because they both knew what was at stake. When her doctor came into the room, instead of introducing himself, he went instead to the computer monitor and brought up Barbara's MRI images. He then turned to Barbara and Bob and said, "You have quite a large mass. There are two types of tumors, benign and malignant. *This looks malignant.*" With that statement, he left the room.

This news was exactly what they had feared. Bob was more devastated than Barbara. "He was very upset!" She tried to comfort him. Surprisingly, she was more concerned about Bob than what this meant for her. After a good fifteen minutes, the doctor returned—he had consulted with another doctor. They had agreed that he needed to operate as soon as she could be scheduled.

Barbara's response was, "Oh no, I can't have any operation. I'm a kindergarten teacher. My angels need to be with me that first day. This is very important. This is the biggest day of their lives."

The doctor's response was direct, "It looks like you won't be starting school this year and you will need to prepare for surgery in two days."

With that statement weighing heavily on them both, they pulled themselves together and left the hospital. When they arrived home, it was time to let the family know the bad news. Barbara called her sister and adult son and daughter. She let them know of the upcoming surgery to remove a mass that extended under her right eye. She told them that the doctors thought it was cancerous.

She admitted that it was difficult to say the word, "cancerous." She asked for their prayers and support, but Barbara could not get herself to call her school principal, even though classes started in less than two weeks. "I was holding off. I just hoped that somehow I would be able to be there for my angels."

The next day, to take their mind off the upcoming surgery, Bob took Barbara on their boat onto Lake Michigan. Once on the water, she had this *terrible thought*, "This might be my last boat ride." The reality of the upcoming surgery was overwhelming her. It was on the boat that she called out to God, "Whatever your plans are for me, I will be okay with it, but I would really like to be with my angels on the first day of school."

At a time like this, you can either be angry with God or accept God's will. The latter is much better and that was the path that Barbara chose.

The next day, the day before the surgery, Barbara received a phone call from her doctor. He said, "I have some news: one of the radiologists at the hospital took a look at your scan and she insists it's dysplasia,[2] *so it's not cancerous after all!*"

Barbara asked, "You mean I can be present the first day of school next week?"

"Yes, there's no reason for you to miss that special day."

All Barbara could say was, "I could not have asked anything more from God, than for me to be present that first day of school with my angels."

PRAISE GOD!

NOTE: After this news, Barbara worked for eleven more years before she retired after a total of thirty-five years of teaching. She now wears a hearing aid that always reminds her of her ordeal years earlier.

Because of her enthusiastic teaching method and friendly calls to her students, they were able to avoid the crying and fear of that first day of school.

——•◄——

[1] An **otoscope** or auriscope is a medical device that is used to look into the ears. Health care providers use otoscopes to screen for illness during regular check-ups and also to investigate ear symptoms. An otoscope potentially gives a view of the ear canal and tympanic membrane or eardrum. (Source: Wikipedia)

[2] **Dysplasia** is a broad term that refers to the abnormal development of cells within tissues or organs. It can lead to a wide range of conditions that involve enlarged tissue or precancerous cells. Developmental dysplasia is common in children and can affect many parts of the body, including the skeleton. (Source: Medical News Today)

CHAPTER 16

Panic

Story from Leona Swaicki of St. Thomas the Apostle Catholic
Church in Glen Mills, PA

*On the third day there was a wedding
in Cana of Galilee, and the mother of Jesus was there.*

JOHN 2:1

LEONA WAS NERVOUS. SHE TOLD herself that she was too
old to be nervous, since she was no kid. She was nearly
fifty years old and *the recital would soon begin.*

She had confidence in her singing ability—it was just the
idea of having to perform in front of an audience. It is one
thing to sing in front of her Japanese voice instructor; it was
quite another thing to sing in front of an audience. To make
matters worse, her instructor wanted her to meet Jerry, another
of her students, a man who was probably about her age. Her
instructor went on to explain that she had already asked him if

he would be willing to meet her. Jerry had said sure, so Leona agreed to meet him.

Her first impression of Jerry was fine, but Leona had other things on her mind, *like the recital*. In another setting, she might have been interested in talking with him, but not at that moment.

Once she was before the audience and began to sing, all tension left her. She was able to depend on her many hours of practice. She was happy when it was over—*she had done it!* She was impressed when Jerry got up to perform his piece, and afterward she found him and congratulated him.

All the participants and their guests went out to dinner to celebrate their successful recital. After a wonderful evening together, people began to leave. It was then that Jerry asked Leona if she could stay to have coffee and talk. She agreed.

They discovered that they had a lot in common: both were Catholic and as kids they had lived within three miles of each other. In fact, Jerry's sisters had attended the same Catholic high school as Leona's brothers. She also learned that Jerry worked nearby. The more they talked, the more it became clear that they enjoyed each other's company. Leona liked Jerry and hoped that they would see more of each other.

Within a month of their recital, Cindy, a long-time friend of Leona, announced that she was getting married. She asked Leona to be one of her bridesmaids. Of course, Leona agreed, since they had been friends for many years.

On the wedding day, they gathered at Cindy's house for pictures. Leona and Cindy's sister were upstairs to help Cindy put on her dress and be there to support her on her big day. Cindy's brother, Jim, was downstairs in the living room with his ten-year-old son, Jeff, who was the ring bearer. (Jim had already given Jeff the box that held the wedding ring.)

The women upstairs were having a fine time, excited that the big day had finally arrived. They all realized that their role in helping Cindy was mostly to be around her to distract her from being nervous—their actual presence and small talk did indeed help calm Cindy. Soon Leona and the other bridesmaids came downstairs to await Cindy. From there they would go by limousine to the church for the wedding.

At one point, Jeff had discovered that the ring was missing from the box. When Jeff told his dad, "The ring is gone," the room became quiet as everyone stopped and looked at Jim and his son. His dad said, "You're teasing me. Don't tease me like that, young man." Panic set in when his son showed him the empty box. Jim appealed to Leona and the rest of the bridal party, *"We have to find the ring before Cindy comes downstairs and discovered that it's missing."*

The entire bridal party began to search the living room for the ring. It had to be there, since Jim had given the ring to Jeff in that room. No one could understand how the ring got out of the box. Jim remembered that Jeff had been chasing the flower girl around the living room earlier; perhaps that's when the ring was lost. If only they could find it in time—Cindy would be coming down the stairs any minute. But they just could not find it. The search continued.

There seems to be a time were panic takes over. You find yourself looking in the same places, as if it will magically appear where it wasn't the first time you looked.

Most had given up looking by now, including Leona, but she felt drawn outside to the deck. She said, "It was there that I verbalized my prayer out load, 'God you have to help us find that ring.' I remember feeling a sense of calm and going back inside. I told Jim that we need to turn the sofa over. He looked at me perplexed. As soon as we turned the sofa over, there was the ring!" Jim picked it up, returned it to the box, and then put it in his pocket. He whispered to Leona, "I'm indebted to you for life."

Almost simultaneously, Cindy appeared at the top of the stairs in her wedding gown and came down the stairs, unaware of what had just taken place; in fact, no one told her until after the wedding.

God had worked through Leona to restore the lost ring. As Leona explained, "A strange calmness came over me after I called out to God and I just knew what to do." Even when Leona helped Jim lift the sofa, it seemed lighter than it should have been.

Praise God!

Leona's story continues in the next chapter.

CHAPTER 17

The Stone Wall

———•———

Story from Leona Swaicki of St. Thomas the Apostle Catholic Church in Glen Mills, PA

Rising very early before dawn, he left and went off to a deserted place, where he prayed.

MARK 1:35

We have our great plans in life, but you can be sure that if we turn to God in prayer, we will discover that His plans are far superior to ours.

This is Leona's story continued from the previous chapter.

THE RECITAL HAD BEEN A great success, but more important was Leona's opportunity to meet Jerry. Leona's life had been focused on her role as a physical therapist (PT) in nursing homes. She would come home from work, walk the dog, fix dinner, and go to bed, only to repeat the sequence the following day. Singing in the choir at church on Sunday had been her only relief from the routine and her demanding role as a PT.

Her desire to do something more had led her to study voice and ultimately to her recital. Now Jerry had entered her life, but she was not thinking about Jerry when she contemplated her vacation. Her idea of vacation was to sleep in and make plans for the day when she woke up.

As it turned out, the morning brought a raw day in March. There was still some ice and snow on the ground, yet it was clear that the spring thaw was well on the way. She decided to make the hour-and-half drive up to the big mall and spend the day browsing and shopping. It would be an all-day event, including lunch at one of the many small restaurants. She was really looking forward to her first day of vacation without a care in the world.

She would soon learn that God had other plans for her that day.

There was a sense of freedom in getting away from work and her regular routine. She thought about meeting Jerry at their voice recital two months earlier. He had asked her out on a few dates, and she had stopped in to visit him at work before attending chorus rehearsals. She said, "I really liked him, and I felt he liked me too, but I was starting to become afraid. I had become convinced that I was going to remain an 'old maid'—I was too old to meet someone and fall in love. I was even considering telling Jerry that I really liked him, but I didn't feel that I could continue to see him."

All these thoughts were going through her mind as she drove on the expressway to the mall. Then she saw the exit sign for 422 West. "I thought, okay, I have passed this sign before on the way to the mall, but something inside of me said to get off at that exit and go instead to the Jesuit retreat house that had been so influential in my life decisions."

She obeyed the inner voice and travelled to the Jesuit retreat house. When she got there, it was very quiet. It was clear that there were no retreats in progress, but she knew that she could walk around and pray.

"I followed one of my favorite paths down to a small pond. Since it was cold and the path somewhat snow covered, I was glad that I had worn my boots and warm jacket. I enjoyed the sound of the wind blowing through the pine trees and the scent of the pines as I walked. I came to the pond and felt an inspiration to sit for a while, but where? Surprisingly, there was one dry spot on the stone wall surrounding the pond. It was as if it was placed there for me."

As Leona sat there, she could see the ice melting on top of the pond and hear the dripping of the melting snow. She noticed the fish that lived in the pond come up to the surface. She felt herself watching the fish and started to tell God how she was feeling. She prayed for how she could tell Jerry how she felt. She was starting to plan how she would tell him that it wasn't him, but that *she was feeling afraid*. It would be much safer to just stay as she was and put all her energy into her work, etc.

"But then, I heard a voice inside me that told me that Jerry and I were meant to meet when we did. Even though we grew up near each other, it had not been the time for us to meet back then. Now was our time—God said that we were meant *to complete* each other."

Leona felt a great sense of calm, "I felt awestruck as I got up and started up the path back to my car. Driving home I couldn't wait until I saw Jerry again."

It was not yet spring, but God had planted love deep in her heart and had made it very clear that He wanted them to be together. All her doubts had evaporated. All plans of the mall were forgotten.

NOTE: Leona and Jerry continued to date, fell in love, and were married eighteen months later. They celebrated their twentieth wedding anniversary on December 16, 2020.

They both agree that it has been the best twenty years of their lives and they thank God each day!

CHAPTER 18

Divine Mercy

———•———

Story from Jennie Buhs of St. Jude's Catholic Church in New Lennox, Illinois

"Lord save me!"
Immediately Jesus stretched out his hand and caught him.

MATHEW 31:30–31

JENNIE SAT WITH THE FAMILY around the dining room table. Her stepbrother, Ray, and her dad were at it again. Ever since Ray became a teenager, he and her dad would debate any issue that Ray felt motivated to bring up, and there were many. Meanwhile, Jennie's brother, Frank Jr. and her stepsister, Debra, ate dinner with their mom, Ruby, in silence.

It had only been recently that Ray had grown a bit rebellious. Frank Sr. was doing his best to firmly defend his position on any of Ray's attacks, but often it was done with a raised voice that tended to silence everyone else at the table. Ray really knew how to get under his stepdad's skin.

Still, it was clear that Frank Sr. loved all the children, even if they weren't all his own.

All four of the children were raised in the Catholic faith through after-school religious education programs. Church on Sunday was not part of the pattern of their family life, since Frank Sr. had to work on Sundays, so neither Ruby, Frank Jr., or Ray went to Mass on Sunday. In fact, only Debra and Jennie attended Mass on a regular basis.

It was much later, when Jennie was in her thirties, that she received a call from Ray. (At that time, he had married and was living in Arizona.) They got into a discussion about their faith. This is how Jennie learned that Ray had become *an atheist*. He said, "When you die, you are going to find out that *there is no God*!" Jennie responded, "But Ray, what if you die and find out that *there is a God*, don't you think you have more to lose?"

Reflecting on their childhood days, she remembered, "Ray never seemed to see the other side of any question." This was no different—he did not respond to Jennie's question.

Throughout the many years following that discussion, this issue never came up again—it was just left there unfinished. Because it was never discussed again, Jennie never knew if Ray had changed his view on his belief in God.

During the years that followed, when the family got together, Ray and Frank Sr.'s relationship improved. They even enjoyed a good laugh. Jennie noticed this change and was happy to see it, both for them and for the family. A better relationship meant a happier time for all.

In August 2006, Jennie's mom, Ruby, died after a long battle with lung cancer. The family gathered at the funeral parlor. Even though Ruby had insisted on a closed casket, Ray would not enter the room but, instead, stayed just outside the room, weeping. Jennie had never seen her older brother cry like that before—he was really upset!

The memorial Mass on the following day was the family's final farewell to their mom. Ray did not sit with the family. He might have been in the back of the church, but none of the family saw him. They all assumed that the funeral Mass was too much for Ray to bear, based on his emotional breakdown the previous night.

A month after Ruby's death, Frank Sr. suffered a stroke and was hospitalized. Two months later, Jennie's younger brother, Frank Jr., received a call from Ray's wife, Cynthia; she told him that Ray had committed suicide sometime in the middle of the night.

Jennie and the family were devastated.

Frank Sr. and Frank Jr. had both received phone calls from Ray the night he had taken his life, but neither had been home to take the call, since they had been out to dinner together. They wondered, "What if I had called him back when I got home—could I have prevented him from taking his life?"

Ray's wife said that she had not seen any warning signs that Ray was in any distress. She did say that Ray had lost his job and he had not been able to find another. The family could only guess what had triggered his suicide, but they realized they would never know.

All Jennie could do was pray for Ray.

Even though she had not been thinking or talking about Ray the day before, about nine years later Jennie had a vivid dream. Jennie explained that she almost never remembers a dream, so she felt that this was a significant dream. "In the dream, I entered a room and there was Ray—with a glowing, loving smile on his face as he looked me in the eye. He came to me and embraced me with love. No words were spoken, and that was the end of the dream."

Jennie felt that Ray was conveying to her that she was right: *there is a God* and Ray was thanking her for praying for him. When Jennie shared her dream with Ray's wife, Cynthia, she said that she too had had a recent dream that Jennie's mom was holding Ray in her arms "cradling him in a loving embrace."

Jennie could only reflect on her discussion with Ray years earlier when they debated what would happen when they died. Jennie had pointed out that Ray had more to lose because he didn't believe in God. What neither of them had counted on was *the mercy of God.*

The Chaplet of Divine Mercy[1] closing prayer:

> *"Eternal God, in whom mercy is endless, and the treasury of compassion inexhaustible, look kindly upon us, and increase Your mercy in us, that in difficult moments we might not despair, nor become despondent, but with great confidence submit ourselves to Your holy will which is love and mercy itself."*

---

[1] **Chaplet of Divine Mercy.** The Chaplet of Divine Mercy was given by Jesus in a vision in 1935 to St. Sister Faustina Kowalska. It takes only ten minutes to pray. It is prayed every day at noon central time on the *Drew Mariani Show*. The chaplet is prayed using rosary beads, with some very beautiful prayers including the *Opening Prayer,* which is as follows: "You expired Jesus, but the source of life gushed forth for souls, and the ocean of mercy opened up for the whole world. O Font of Life, unfathomable Divine Mercy, envelop the whole world and empty yourself out upon us" (Diary 1319).

For the full Chaplet see www.thedivinemercy.org/message/devotions/praythechaplet.php

CHAPTER 19

Roses in November

——◦·•·◦——

Story from Deborah St. Clair of St. Joseph's Catholic Church
in Spreckels, California

Now it is impossible to please God without faith,
because to even approach God you have to believe God exists
and that He rewards those who seek him.

HEBREWS 11:6

SOMETHING MADE DEBORAH TURN AND look toward the
back of the church. She saw her dad among the congregation. Surprised, she thought, "How can he be here? I
thought he was on his deathbed back East."

Deborah was raised with her younger brother in a family very
different than most. Her dad was an atheist, and her mom
was a non-practicing Protestant. Catholics were despised just
for being Catholic, so it created an anti-Catholic atmosphere
in the household.

Her dad was in the armed services, and for that reason, the family moved often. When Deborah was in middle school, they moved to New Jersey into a Catholic neighborhood.

Mary's gift of the rosary to us is life changing, and it provides a direct link to God.

There was something about her Catholic neighbors that appealed to her. She doesn't remember how she came to have a rosary, but she began to pray the rosary often. Her prayers must have been fruitful, because she soon made the decision that she wanted *to become Catholic.*

At a nearby Catholic church, she mustered enough courage to tell a priest that she wanted to become Catholic. He told her that because she was only fifteen, she would need to have her parent's permission. She knew that this would be a problem. It took even more courage to ask her father for his permission. Her father said emphatically, "NO!" He went on to explain that *anyone who believes in God is an idiot.*

This statement had a major impact on her life.

Deborah loved her father and she certainly didn't want to be considered an idiot, so she did a complete reversal and became, as she described, a "raging atheist." This change did not manifest itself in conflicts with classmates, because Deborah by nature was a quiet, perhaps even withdrawn, young teenager; but she did carry hostility toward anything to do with Christianity. She had accepted completely her father's belief that *Christians were dumb.*

When Deborah was twenty-seven, her mom died. She realized that she was on her own, especially since she rarely saw her dad anymore. She found that her life was slipping away—she worked all week and on weekends she did laundry and cleaned her apartment. So, before she knew it, Deborah was in her early forties, dealing with *depression*. She began seeing a psychiatrist, who expressed concern for the balance in her life. He said that perhaps her depression was linked to diet, so he sent her to a nutritionist.

The nutritionist explained to Deborah, "You are taking care of your psychological life with the help of a psychiatrist, your physical life through exercise, but what about your spiritual life?" When Deborah explained her atheist attitude, her nutritionist recommended that she read, *Mere Christianity*. She told her that the author, C. S. Lewis, is one of the most profound writers and intellects of all time, and the book is *a classic*.

The effect of *Mere Christianity* on Deborah was profound. As she explained, "Once I had read *Mere Christianity*, it was a done deal after that." She thought of all the years wasted. She recalled her childhood desire to become a Catholic and her father's attack on all Christians. Deborah realized that God had been pursuing her for as long as she could remember.

It was time for her to yield to God and become Catholic.

Deborah enrolled in the RCIA[1] program at St. Jude's Catholic Church in Marina, California. She became part of the RCIA candidate group. It was like a big family, thirty-two in number:

those pursuing baptism or confirmation or both. There were also sponsors from the parish for each candidate. Even the sponsors learned more about their faith at those weekly meetings.

Deborah found herself looking forward to the meetings.

Each Sunday before being dismissed, they would sit together at Mass until after the Scripture readings and homily. They would then move to the hall to discuss the readings for the day. At set times throughout the year, they would be part of ceremonies during Mass in front of the congregation.

In November, there is the Rite of Acceptance.[2] On that day, as part of the ceremony, all the inquirers and candidates were spread out down the church aisles. The priest made the sign of the cross on them and prayed over them. Then the congregation was asked for their acceptance of the candidates and inquirers. Applause followed as a sign of their support.

It was at this time that Deborah felt moved to look over her shoulder at the congregation. This is when she spotted her father in the assembly. Her gasp went unnoticed, but she was visibly shaken. The ceremony was soon over. Deborah and the others exited the church to gather and discuss the readings. They did not stay for the Liturgy of the Eucharist—that would not be allowed until the Easter Vigil, when they would be baptized and confirmed.

When Deborah's group was dismissed, she rushed back into the church to find her father. She checked the side doors and the front of the church, *but he was gone.* She returned to her sponsor, disappointed. She thought it was strange—why would he come and yet not stay to greet her?

After Mass, Deborah, her sponsor, and the others drove to the Carmelite Monastery, which is south of Carmel, overlooking the ocean. Even though this was a November morning, Deborah was overwhelmed by the smell of roses. She mentioned it to her sponsor, who did not share her experience, since there were no roses in bloom at that time of year.

After the visit to the Carmelite Monastery, they all went out for breakfast. Later, they visited San Carlos Cathedral, where Deborah again experienced a strong smell of roses. Deborah's comment about the scent of roses seemed to have become a slight annoyance to her sponsor. Finally, Deborah went home, only to discover a call from her brother on her answering machine. The message was brief. Her father had died at 10:15 that morning. Deborah immediately realized that he had died about the same time that she had seen him at St. Jude's Church. *She was stunned.*

This was a lot to take in for Deborah. Looking back on her life with her father, she remembered that he had dismissed her interest in the Catholic Church not only when she was fifteen, but again when she told him that she was joining the RCIA program to become Catholic. Yet there he was in church on the day of the Rite of Acceptance. She also wondered what the smell of roses meant. It was as if he were saying to her, I want you to know I love you and I support your desire to become Catholic.

It was months later that Deborah was baptized and received into the Church at the Easter Vigil Mass at St. Jude's Catholic Church. At that time, she still struggled with the "Real Presence" of Christ in the Eucharist, but when she stood up to go up to receive First Holy Communion, her knees buckled. She said, "I felt that Mary and Jesus were present with me." After receiving Holy Communion, she returned to her pew knowing that Christ was truly present within her.

Her entrance into the Church was complete. For the next month, "Every time I went to Communion, I was just a crying blubbering fool, but I couldn't help it."

Finally, in the days that followed, Deborah learned that the *fragrance of roses* is always associated with the presence of our Blessed Mother. Mary had come to her that day at the Carmelite Monastery and at San Carlos Cathedral—on the same day that she had seen her father in the congregation.

Mary and Jesus had truly been with her all the way up to her First Communion and they are still with her today.

---

[1] **RCIA** (The Rite of Christian Initiation of Adults) is a process developed by the Catholic Church for prospective converts to Catholicism who are above the age of infant baptism. Candidates are introduced to aspects of Catholic beliefs and practices over a six-month or longer period of weekly small-group meetings with other interested prospective converts, as well as members of the parish who act as sponsors. Guest speakers are often local priests or the pastor of the parish. During this period, close friendships are built that provide a sense of community and welcoming, as well as period of openness to learn about the Catholic Church.

[2] **The Rite of Acceptance** into the Order of Catechumens (Rite of Acceptance) is the first of the "threshold rites" of the Rite of Christian Initiation of Adults (RCIA), and the first public ritual. In the Rite of Acceptance, a change of identity takes place: those previously known as inquirers become catechumens. They are officially welcomed by the Church as disciples, members (albeit not yet full members) of the household of faith. The text calls this rite "the first consecration by the Church" for those seeking Christian initiation. They are literally marked with the cross of Christ as God's own. (Source: The Introduction to the Rite of Acceptance into the Order of Catechumens and the Rite of Welcoming the Candidates)

CHAPTER 20

The Power of Prayer

———•———

Story from Tom and Lois Lukes of Our Lady of Mount Carmel in Carmel Valley, CA

Whatever you ask for in prayer with faith you will receive.

MATTHEW 21:22

THERE IS A TIME THAT comes for many of us where, out of desperation, we turn to *prayer*. This happened to my wife, Lois, and me in our ninth year of our marriage. The only problem was that we were in such bad straits that we didn't know *what to pray for*. I later realized that that didn't matter—God was very capable of dealing with that too.

It all began a year and a half earlier when I went into a partnership with a house developer. I was the architect, while he was to find the investors and deal with getting the bank loans to build the large custom homes. One year later, his money had run out. Although I had done the drawings for three houses, money was tight, and the banks were not loaning on "home construction" projects. My partner said we would just have to wait for the banks to open up loans again, but I had a family to feed—I couldn't wait.

With little money in the bank to continue, I left the partnership. I felt that I had done my part, but my partner had not done his. I still went in the office to do what I could to wrap up the last project, but without pay. I was still paying staff half of their salary, and my partner paid the other half.

Lois and I had made a Marriage Encounter[1] two years earlier and we were part of a "Love Circle" in which three couples met every week to support each other. We shared our dilemma with these close friends and asked them to pray for guidance to help us know what to do. Should I look for a job, work from home on my own, try to resurrect the original partnership . . . or what? They all shared ideas, but none really helped.

They all promised to pray for us each day.

It was about that time that I had a serious back spasm attack in the downtown parking lot at work. I thought that this was the last thing I needed. (God knew otherwise.) My back pain was so bad that I struggled to even get into my car, since I was locked up in pain.

When I got home, I struggled to get in bed. I kept my knees bent and my upper back flat on the bed. My wife, Lois, was home with our two boys Michael (age six) and Tim (age four.)

For two days I lay there, unable to do much of anything, although a hot shower did help. On the third day, Lois came in to keep me company and sat on the edge of the bed reading the morning paper. We talked about our dilemma as she glanced at the *Los Angeles Times*.

Unknown to me, she was flipping through the classified section. She said, "Listen to this: Central California architect looking for licensed architect to run his office; must have experience in running an office . . . " I thought, "Central California, that sounds like Bakersfield or Fresno—both hot climate cities—maybe this was not a good idea." I added, "And I'm not even looking for a job." But I had to agree with Lois that it might be the answer to our prayers, and I certainly met the job requirements.

Sitting up in bed, I wrote a "hand printed" resume as neatly as I could. (We didn't have a typewriter.) We mailed it off the next day to a Los Angeles address. My attitude was: what do I have to lose? It was almost a "lark." Within a week, my back had recovered, and I heard from the contact in Los Angeles by phone. He said that I was one of two architects selected to be interviewed. I asked, "Where is the job in Central California? He said, "Salinas." (Salinas is not in central California, it is in the "central coast.")

This was sounding better all the time!

We had even driven through Salinas on our way to Carmel for our honeymoon nine years earlier. Salinas was only twenty miles from one of the most beautiful coastlines in the country! I was excited. My parents offered to watch our two boys and pay for our airfare to San Jose, the car rental, and the motel, because by now, we did not have the money to cover any of these costs.

As it turned out, I learned that the firm was highly respected in the area. They did all the work for the Salinas junior college, as well as most of the banks in town. I saw it as a great opportunity, if only I were selected. The interview went well, but the architect/owner was not a very warm person. I was a little concerned what it would be like to work for him.

Lois and I had a lot to discuss. Our families lived in Pasadena and Los Angeles. This job would mean selling our house and leaving our families. (For a young couple with two young boys, having the help of grandparents is a big factor to consider.)

I decided to leave it up to God. If God opened the door, then I would follow. If it didn't work out, I could always seek employment elsewhere. So, we headed to Salinas.

That Sunday, we went to church at San Carlos Cathedral Church in Monterey. *It was Pentecost Sunday, the birthday of the Church.*

During the Mass, we were overwhelmed by the beauty of the old mission-like church. We learned that it was built in 1794 even before the Carmel Mission. The homily that day was powerful—matching the importance of the feast day. Afterward, Lois said she felt that the priest was looking right at her—he was speaking to her. If this was part of our answer from God, we thought that the fact that it was Pentecost was important. It seemed that God was pointing the way, that this was His plan. Now, I need to be selected.

Our answer came the following week, when I was notified that *I had been selected for the job!*

By now, we were committed to going, but I made an offer to go up to Salinas and work for three months to try out the job and give them an opportunity to see whether I met their qualifications. The architect agreed.

After the first week in the new job, I learned that I was correct in my initial assessment. This firm would be a great opportunity, but the boss would be difficult to work for. I was committed to trying, but in the meantime, I found a firm in Monterey that offered me a position as well. I now had a backup plan, if I had problem dealing with the architect who had hired me in Salinas.

I finished up my three-month trial period. We decided that we wanted to move up to Salinas, but the job itself might not work out. Still, as long as I had another job lined up, we would be fine.

My new boss gave me time to sell my house and find a new one in Salinas, but that was more difficult than I thought. Lois and I had made an offer on a house, but it fell through. I had to find a house during the three-month trial period without Lois's input. I found a nice four-bedroom house in a five-hundred home development called Toro Park on the highway between Salinas and Monterey. They accepted our offer.

On December 22, we left Pasadena for Salinas with the movers already on the road ahead of us. Lois drove the VW square-back with Tim, our youngest, and our cat, Ike. I had Michael in our Toyota Celica and our dog, Tina.

It soon became clear that this would not be an ordinary seven-hour trip. The problem was that at that time of year, Interstate 5 can be dangerous. This became obvious when we started down the steep north side of the highway. Snow and rain came just as we hit the low fog. Visibility was about the length of a semi-truck.

All the eighteen wheelers were in the slow lane, forming a wall moving at a fair pace down in the fog, rain, and snow. We were driving together in the lane next to the line of huge trucks. I decided to pull in front of Lois, so that she could follow my taillights in the fog.

This didn't work because I soon lost sight of her. I tried to maintain the same speed as the trucks, but it must have been too fast for Lois.

By the bottom-third of the descent, we were out of the fog and snow, but Lois was nowhere to be seen. I pulled over half a mile from the bottom and waited. Ten or fifteen minutes later, Lois pulled up behind me. She was *quite upset* by the traumatic descent. She said, "I really didn't think I was going to make it."

I tried to explain my strategy to lead her down the mountain, but she wouldn't hear it. *So far, our new life in Salinas was not going very well* and we weren't even there yet. This was a very bad start, but it would get worse when Lois saw the house that I had purchased.

When we finally arrived in Salinas, some seven hours after we started, we stopped by the empty house—our house. The owner was still there wiping down the kitchen cabinet shelves.

The living room had a bare Christmas tree in the corner, but that did not overcome the bare walls, empty rooms, and pale-green carpet. The long day and the fog experience didn't help either. *Lois was not happy.* It was twenty-two degrees outside and all the shrubs in the yard had died from two weeks of record subfreezing nights. This was the end of a rough day.

We spent the night three blocks away with Paul and Margaret Danielson,[2] a local Episcopal minister and friend of Lois's family in Los Angeles. (They were the ones who had placed the Christmas tree in our living room to brighten the house as a welcome.)

We had traveled a long way, only to find a house that needed lots of work, but our new friends, the Danielsons, did their best to share the Christmas spirit with us. We had to stop and be grateful that we had safely made the trip, we had new friends, and I had a job.

Within the next six years, a lot happened: we found a wonderful church (St. Joseph's), remodeled our house, attended a Cursillo[3] weekend and I had become a partner in an architectural firm in Salinas. Most importantly, we had our third son, Stephen.[4] In addition, God had placed us in a beautiful part of California with a mild climate. We loved what God had done for us when we didn't know what to pray for.

I must admit that it wasn't until we made Cursillo five years after we arrived in Salinas that I was able to see God's hand in answering our prayer. We had been so wrapped up in the interview, finding a house, the new job, etc., that I had failed to thank God for answering our prayers.

Looking back on how God answered our prayers and our friends' prayers was amazing. Out of the blue, God sent me a back spasm so that I would be home for Lois to read the ad in the *LA Times* for a job that was exactly suited for my background. He brought us to an area of the state that we had not even considered . . . where we had honeymooned. But God also brought us into a faith community centered on Him through the Cursillo movement. And eventually, He called me to write the *GOD Incidents* series of books that shares God's goodness with the readers. PRAISE GOD!

NOTE: I never had back problems before this episode, but it started a series of events that changed our lives forever.

————— • —————

[1] **Marriage Encounter** is a Catholic process that married couples *of all faiths* can experience over a two-day weekend. The weekend gives spouses an opportunity to grow in their marriage through open and honest communication, face-to-face

sharing, and heart-to-heart encounter in a comfortable, relaxed setting. Marriage Encounter invites and encourages married couples of all ages and faith expressions to share in this experience and to become an integral part of this journey" (National Marriage Encounter website, http://marriage-encounter.org/). See chapter 18 of *God Incidents—True Stories of God Working in the Lives of Catholics (Book 1)* to read, "Our Encounter" that was the author's encounter with God that changed his life.

[2] In **Paul Danielson's** story titled, *The Visions* in *GOD Incidents—True Stories of God Working in the Lives of Catholics* (Book 1), Paul shares his conversion story that led him from being an Episcopal priest to became Catholic.

[3] **Cursillo** (cur-see-yo) is a Roman Catholic movement that was founded in Majorca, Spain, in 1944 as a three-day weekend retreat for men to prepare them to participate in the Camino de Santiago pilgrimage. It was also intended to bring the men back to the Church. It came to Texas in 1959 and California in 1962 and it quickly spread throughout the USA.

Cursillo has been declared by the Catholic Church as a charism of the Holy Spirit. It was so successful that the women insisted on being included. Later, the Catholics invited their Christian brothers and sisters to join them. Eventually, Catholics and other Christian faiths split into separate weekends—one Catholic and one Anglican.

Cursillo consists of a series of short talks given by the lay team members and one or more priests who act as spiritual directors. The men attend on one weekend, with the women attending the following weekend. The candidates and team arrive on Thursday after work, but the Cursillo formally begins on Friday. The three-day experience ends Sunday afternoon.

[4] **Stephen**. In *GOD Incidents II—More True Stories of God Working in the Lives of Catholics*, Chapter 11, "It's the Water," describes Stephen's birth and Lois's serious pregnancy issues.

CHAPTER 21

Miraculous Cross

———•———

Story from Joseph Vespalec of St. Frances Cabrini Catholic Church in West Bend, WI

Your brother was dead and has come to life again;
he was lost and has been found.

LUKE 15:32

There are times in life when we make mindless choices
that lead us away from God. We may not intend to
do so, but soon we have traveled along a different path
than when we started. It is amazing that God continues
to work in our lives to help us find our way back to
Him. This is Joe's story.

JOE GREW UP IN A large Catholic family. He was the seventh child of eight—four boys and four girls. There are always benefits of a large family. As Joe put it, "Being the youngest boy allowed me to learn from my brothers' mistakes." Joe's father was a great influence on the family. On family vacations, he would always find a Catholic church for the family to attend.

Joe always felt his dad was the rock of the family's faith. Years after Joe married and moved away from the family, that strong family faith was shattered when Joe's older brother Johnny was killed in a car accident on a stormy night in 1996.

Johnny's death devastated the family and caused so much grief that Joe's parents became angry with God and stopped attending church. This affected Joe and his family as well—Joe's father no longer thought church was important, so Joe drifted away from church attendance as well. For Joe, it was not a decision out of anger toward God, but rather a combination of things: he was older now, and did not feel close to God—he did not have a relationship with God. So, when his mom and dad stopped going to church, it was easy for Joe to do the same.

By the time of Johnny's death, Joe was married to Andrea. Their son Matthew had been baptized, but that was when the family was still attending church. With Johnny's death, everything changed. It was not that Joe had abandoned God—Joe still found time to pray to God, but God was no longer part of Joe's family's life.

You might say that Joe could no longer say that God was important. Looking back on it today, Joe admits, "I never really let God into my life." In fact, when Joe and all his high school class went on their confirmation retreat and eventually were confirmed, Joe decided not to be confirmed. This decision would later turn out to be significant in the life and growth of his own family.

Joe's second son, Brett, was born in 1998, much to the delight of the family. Matthew had a little brother and Joe and his wife had their second child to raise and love. Since they no longer attended Mass, Brett was not baptized. Over time this began to gnaw at Joe. "I always feared that I would not see Brett baptized before I died."

Time was slipping away, and Joe did nothing to change the family's spiritual life.

When Joe's father was dying in 2009, the family gathered around his hospital bed. His father's sister, Aunt Rosemary, and her husband, Uncle Dick, were there as well. Aunt Rosemary asked the family if they would like to all say a rosary for their father. (The family had never said a rosary as a family before, but they all wanted to do this for their dad.) When the rosary was finished, Joe's dad had a slight body movement and slipped away a short time later. The family felt that they had helped him with their prayers.

Praying the rosary as a family was the beginning of the family reaching out to God after being away for so long. Little steps are often necessary to open the doors to embrace God's grace.

September 12, 2012, on Friday at 1 p.m., Joe was terminated at Coca-Cola where he had worked for twenty-six years. *Joe was devastated.* He had not seen this coming. "It was the longest drive home in my life."

Now he had to face his wife and tell her the bad news.

Joe was the sole supporter of the family. He realized that he was in a bad state—at age forty-seven he knew that he was no longer a young man; he did not have a college degree, but he still had his faith.

Joe did not know where to even start. What type of job should he pursue? It was time to turn to God. He prayed to God, "Help me find a job *that I can do.*"

Things were starting to happen, like a snowball rolled in the snow—it starts small, but it quickly gets bigger and bigger.

His resume had been sent out, but Joe was struggling with his job fears. He thought, "Who would want to hire me?" He took a walk and asked God for direction in his life. Joe paused in his walk and looked down. On the sidewalk right in front of him was a silver Miraculous Cross.[1] Joe bent down and picked it up.

He knew that this was for him from God. The cross united Mary's Miraculous Medal image with the image of the Sacred Heart of Jesus in the form of a cross. The cross also included a dove and the figure of his namesake, St. Joseph, carrying Baby Jesus. It was clear to Joe that *help was on the way.*

A few weeks later, out of the blue, Brett approached Joe, "Dad, I want to be baptized." Joe did not know what had motivated his son, but faith was returning to his family. Things were starting to happen.

After dropping off Brett at his job at McDonald's on Sunday, Joe felt moved to go to Mass at St. Frances Cabrini—it was just a spontaneous impulse. Joe expected that nothing had changed in the twenty-five years since he last stepped into a Catholic church, but he was wrong. *He liked the changes.*

The following Sunday, he decided to return. After Mass was over, Joe approached the celebrant with this plea, "Father, I need help." He then briefly explained his years away from the Church and his desire to return, as well as Brett's desire to be baptized. The priest, Fr. Nathan, suggested that Joe make an appointment so that Joe could explain his situation in more detail. After leaving the church, Joe drove to the store in tears. "I was literally crying uncontrollably. I knew that I had done the right thing." *The snowball was growing larger.*

Joe's meeting the following week with Fr. Nathan was amazing. Father suggested that Joe, his wife, and his boys all attend RCIA, which would culminate at the Easter Vigil Mass in Brett's baptism, First Holy Communion, and confirmation for Brett and the rest of the family. Joe eagerly agreed. Now the family would be united in a walk of faith for the next six months. (Matthew was nineteen and Brett was fourteen.)

Aunt Rosemary and Uncle Dick agreed to sponsor Joe and Andrea and be godparents for Brett at his baptism. This seemed appropriate, since they were the ones who had suggested the rosary at Joe's dad's hospital bedside—when the family first turned back to God. *God's plan was unfolding.*

Within weeks of Joe's return to the Church, he was contacted by a computer repair and maintenance company. After the interview, he was hired to manage their staff. Joe still can't explain how they got his resume, but he knows that God was certainly behind it.

Before the Easter Vigil Mass, Joe made his first confession in more than twenty-six years. "It was long and one that I will never forget." The return to the Church of his youth was nearly complete. Joe realized that his high school decision not to receive confirmation with his classmates now allowed him to receive this sacrament with his family, which made it even more special.

So, when Easter Vigil arrived on March 30, 2013, the Vespalec family stood together and officially came back to the Church— Matthew made his First Communion, Brett was baptized and made his First Communion, and all four of the family were confirmed.

As Joe described it, "It was the best night of my life."

PRAISE GOD!

[1] The image of the Miraculous Cross that Joe found on the sidewalk, which he still wears today.

CHAPTER 22

Lost

———•———

Story from John Candela of Our Lady of the Blessed Sacrament
Catholic Church in Bayside, NY

> *Rejoice with me because I have found the coin that I have lost,*
> *In just the same way, I tell you, there will be rejoicing among*
> *the angels over one sinner who repents.*

LUKE 15:9-10

JOHN'S COMPANY AGREED TO TRANSFER him to Houston,
Texas, to allow him to be with his wife, Patrice, who was
finishing her graduate studies.

When their first child, Angela, was born, the young couple
was faced with a new dilemma. Although Patrice had worked
diligently to qualify for medical school, she was now having
second thoughts. In fact, she had doctor friends warn her that
it is difficult to raise children and be a doctor. They told her,
"One or the other will suffer." So, John and Patrice decided

to drop the idea of medical school for Patrice, but rather focus on raising a family.

While they lived in Houston, they met many evangelical Christians. John described these evangelical as "joyful and friendly." Although John and Patrice were greatly affected by these friends, they never attended any of their church services. However, they did begin to question why their Catholic parish members did not exhibit the same enthusiasm and joy.

Once Patrice finished her graduate degree, they moved back to New York, where they had grown up and could be close to their families. They naturally took this joyful and friendly attitude of their evangelical friends and carried it with them into their Catholic parish. They thought that perhaps this attitude would influence their new parish community.

They settled in Bayside, Queens, a borough of New York City about twenty-five miles from the coast. Over the next fifteen years, they were blessed with four more children: Andrew, Nicholas, Joseph, and Juliana. Schooling their children turned out to be a challenge, since Andrew had a severe peanut allergy. Faced with this danger and some questionable subject matter being taught, John and Patrice decided to have Patrice homeschool their children. Their homeschooling extended through eighth grade. Patrice's decision to drop her medical career to stay home and raise their children proved to be the right decision.

While Patrice was busy raising the five children, John was out working to support the family. The distance to John's work forced him to drive nearly an hour each way. He used this time to listen to "Christian radio." John liked hearing Chuck Swindoll, Charles Stanley, and other shows, but he sometimes found the shows contrary to Catholic teaching. It was on one of these days in 2014 that John became frustrated with that day's broadcast. He decided to turn the dial, hoping to find something else.

Much to his surprise, he came across a channel that was discussing Catholic principles—he had accidentally found *Relevant Radio.*[1] His first thought was, "What is this? I couldn't believe what I was hearing! I had never heard Catholic radio before." He was overjoyed to finally hear the truth of his faith shared on a national radio show. The influence of his evangelical friends in Houston had led him first to Christian radio and then indirectly to Catholic radio and with it a life-changing experience that continues to this day. Now John had a new reason to be joyful. A new chapter in his life had begun.

It was on the Friday of Labor Day weekend 2016 that Patrice called John at work. She suggested that since he was scheduled to leave early that day, he should meet them at the beach. (They had not been to the beach all summer.)

John was delighted with the suggestion since he and the family loved the beach. As John described it, "The beach is special: the sky, water, and sand. It is a place where you can unplug." It was late in the afternoon when he arrived to join Patrice and their two youngest children: Joseph (age, thirteen) and Juliana (age, nine). His daughter had also invited her friend Hannah to join them.

After slipping off his shoes, John decided to walk along the water's edge in his bare feet, looking for small colorful stones and shells. The feeling of the water running over his feet and ankles was relaxing and the rhythm of the waves was hypnotic. He loved the beach.

John was rinsing off the sand from some pretty little stones that he had picked up, when it happened—right below him in the wet sand he saw his wedding ring. It must have slipped off from the cold water when he rinsed off the sand from his fingers. In that moment of hesitation, the water from the next wave slipped between his feet and covered the ring just as he lunged for it. He came up with nothing but sand.

As the water receded, John saw that *the ring was gone*!

Instinctively, John grabbed at the sand where the ring had been, but without success. He called out to his family for help. "I've lost my ring! Come and help me!" The family quickly joined in the search.

The waves continued to wash over his feet and ankles as John searched for the missing wedding ring. He was convinced that it must be near where he was standing unless it had been pulled out into the ocean. But no, it had to be close by.

They all continued to search while the waves rhythmically washed across his feet. He stayed close to where the ring had been seen last. He couldn't understand how it could have disappeared so quickly. He had been standing right where the waves ended, so there was little depth to the water—just wet sand and then water from the wave. John thought, *"Some guy with one of those metal detectors will probably find it!"*

Finally, after ten minutes of searching, John raised his eyes and looked up into the sky.

It was late in the day. The sun was low in the sky, which had changed to a beautiful orange with highlighted broken clouds. John was moved to pray, "Mother Mary, you know I am not a man who cares about material things, but you know what this ring symbolizes for me. If you could, would you please help me find the ring?

"I looked down at my feet, and I swear, it was right there—it wasn't even buried. It was just resting there on the wet sand. With another wave on the way, I dove down, grabbed a handful of sand with the ring. The water washed over my feet, I opened my hand, and it was there!"

John called out to his family, "I FOUND IT!"

When his family gathered around him, his daughter Juliana announced, "I said two Hail Marys for you." Not to be outdone, Joseph said, "I prayed to St. Anthony, my *go-to saint.*" At that moment, John felt united with his family and God. *He thanked God for this little miracle.* He knew it was more than a ring. It represented his marriage and family to him.

Mary had come through again! The ring was soon back on John's finger as he embraced his wife and children with pure joy! PRAISE GOD!

—————•—————

[1] **Relevant Radio**® is a Catholic radio network mainly broadcasting talk radio and religious programming. It is the largest Catholic radio network in the United States. There are 185 stations spread throughout thirty-nine states. The Mass, the rosary, and the Chaplet of Divine Mercy are said every day. (Source: Wikipedia) Find a station where you live: https://relevantradio.com/listen/stations/ or you can listen live using the Relevant Radio App at the App Store.

CHAPTER 23

Blackout

Story from Giovanni of San Carlos Cathedral Catholic Church in Monterey, California

For I know well the plans I have for you says the Lord,
plans for your welfare, not for woe!
plans to give you a future full of hope.

JEREMIAH 29:11

Often, we question why events happen to us, not under-
standing God's purpose behind them.

THE CAR HAD FINALLY COME to rest, but its shape had been greatly distorted by the impact of the crash. Anyone seeing the damaged car would have thought that the driver had been killed. When the fire department arrived, they could see the still form of the driver beneath the air bag. They only hoped they could reach him in time. Using the "Jaws of

Life," they cut the door off the mangled car body. Much to their surprise, the driver, although unconscious, was alive.

Giovanni awoke in the emergency room of the nearest trauma center hospital, unaware of what had happened or even how he got there. The doctor explained to him what he had learned of the terrible accident. He was surprised to discover that his patient knew nothing of the accident. At first, the doctor thought Giovanni's memory loss was due to the trauma of the accident, but after various tests and an MRI, he could see it was something else.

Giovanni had a colloidal cyst on his brain and a buildup of fluids caused by the cyst. The doctor stated that it was a life-threatening situation that needed *immediate* surgery. The doctor concluded that this mass and the related fluids were what caused the accident—Giovanni had simply blacked out because of the pressure on his brain.

The prospect of brain surgery was frightening, but Giovanni knew that his recovery depended on the success of the surgery. He was just grateful that his condition might be relieved through surgery.

His wife arrived at the hospital, only to learn that her husband was not injured in the accident, but now faced brain surgery. For both Giovanni and his wife, the thought of him undergoing brain surgery was unsettling. It raised many questions: would the surgery be successful? Would Giovanni have a normal life afterward or could he even die if it were unsuccessful?

Even with fears of the upcoming surgery, Giovanni thought about the two accidents in which he had been involved in the previous three months. He had even received a letter warning that if he had another accident, the DMV would suspend his license. He realized that this was the least of his concerns right then—he needed to focus on calming down his wife and praying that God would help him through this operation—at least it was operable!

"As I was being given general anesthesia, I prayed that God would make the surgery successful and give me a chance to live again. *God gave me the inner peace* that I needed."

The result of the surgery was great news—the cyst had been surgically removed and with it the related buildup of fluids. The neurosurgeon told Giovanni and his wife that it was possible that the cyst might return, so he would need to have an MRI in one month, in six months, one year, and finally in two years. Again, Giovanni prayed to God for help that the cyst would not return.

Amazingly, within two weeks Giovanni was able to return to work and resume a normal life. The DMV never suspended his driver's license, much to his surprise.

The accident had been horrific, but fortunately no one had been injured. More importantly, it called to light that Giovanni had been a *walking time bomb*—the accident saved Giovanni's life, since he might have died if the cyst had not been discovered and treated.

Giovanni calls the event and the surgery that followed *a miracle*. It is clear that God was looking out for him on that day.

NOTE: It has been more than twenty-five years since the surgery and the cyst has not returned. PRAISE GOD!

CHAPTER 24

Two Lepers

—·—

Story from Kramer Soderberg of Holy Family Catholic Church in Decatur, Illinois

*For this I was born and for this I came into the world,
to testify to the truth. Everyone who belongs
to the truth listens to my voice.*

JOHN 18:37

"WHEN I LOOKED DOWN AT my arms—they were covered with open sores and peeling skin. *I realized that I was a leper.*"

Kramer's father, Brad, was a college basketball coach, so it was not a surprise that their family life revolved around basketball. Kramer's mom, Linda, was the anchor of the family. She raised their three children: Kramer, the oldest; his sister, Daley; and the younger brother, Davis.

Although Brad was gone many nights coaching, he made a point to take his family to Mass every Sunday. He made sure that all the kids attended Catholic grade school to help in their Catholic formation. Daily Mass and Adoration were a major part of Brad's life, which did not go unnoticed by Kramer.

The true test of a father's influence can only be seen later when his children leave home and make their own decision to continue to pursue God through the Catholic Church, or simply abandon their faith.

Coaching on the college level greatly affected Kramer's family, since job changes were not only often, but also meant moving to other cities or even other states—very much like families with a father in the armed forces. In the Soderberg's case, the family moved from Iowa to South Dakota, then to Wisconsin and later to Missouri, all to follow his dad's job as a college coach.

Kramer took to basketball as any natural athlete would, but with his father to help he developed into an outstanding high school star. In his senior year, Kramer was named "Missouri High School Player of the Year." Throughout high school, he attended Mass every Sunday with his parents, but he really felt nothing special in that experience—he was just going through the motions, while being obedient to his parents. Kramer did not know Jesus, except as a figure who he heard about at church, not a real person whom he could relate to.

Kramer's life was focused on basketball.

By the time Kramer was a senior in high school, his goal was to play basketball for a Division 1 university coached by his dad. But after his junior year of high school, his dad lost his job as head coach at St. Louis University, so Kramer was forced to change his plans. Fortunately, he was awarded a scholarship to Miami of Ohio University, a Division I school.

For Kramer, college life brought with it new challenges—it was the first time he was away from home on his own. Basketball may have been his focus, but now he had to follow his faith or go it alone. He chose to dig deep and he discovered through months of study a personal relationship with Jesus that the Catholic Church was the true church Christ founded.

After two years at Miami of Ohio, his dad was hired as head coach at Lindenwood University in St. Charles, Missouri, so Kramer transferred there in order to be coached by his dad.

During his last two years of college, he rekindled his relationship with Andrea, who he had known in sixth grade at St. Cletus Catholic grade school. After graduating college, Kramer was hired by Lindenwood University as an assistant coach under his dad. After his first year of coaching, he married Andrea. As Kramer put it, "Apparently, even in sixth grade we knew that we were made for each other."

After coaching with his son for three years, Kramer's dad was offered an assistant coaching position at the University of Virginia. This was great news that the family all celebrated, because it was a real step up to a Division 1 school for his father. However, this promotion brought with it a crisis for Kramer and his family.

With his dad's departure, all of Brad's staff lost their jobs, including Kramer. This was in June, which was a tough time for a coach to be looking for a job. This reality was soon apparent to Kramer and his family, because no one was interested in hiring him.

Kramer and Andrea had recently purchased a home, so they had a mortgage they had to pay. They had a little boy named Krayton, which meant another mouth to feed. Their sole income was from his wife's job, which paid little. However, Kramer did now have his faith to sustain him and, hopefully, carry him through this crisis.

He turned in prayer to Jesus. By July, he had started a journal to just express his thoughts during this period. Some of the entries were reflections on his frustrations—why me? Why now? But he did write this:

> *"What joy and peace I would find if every thought, word, and action were based on the realization that God is always with me and loves me more than anything in the world. I'll keep trying. . ."*

Other entries reflected on daily devotional readings that had touched him including this reading from Mark's Gospel:

> *A leper came to him [and kneeling down] begged him and said, "If you wish, you can make me clean." Moved with*

> *pity, he stretched out his hand, touched him, and said to him, "I do will it. Be made clean." (Mark 1:40–41)*

Kramer realized that *he himself felt like a leper*—he was isolated from work; no one seemed to want to hire him, almost as if something was wrong with him. He was down in the dumps . . . he definitely felt low. What was he to do?

His job options were quickly diminishing. He was ready to give up when *it happened.* In late September, Millikin University in Decatur, Illinois, called and expressed interest in him. After an interview, he was hired as an assistant coach. God had come through, even though Kramer himself had all but given up.

But there is definitely more to this story.

It was four years later that Kramer's brother, Davis, began experiencing *anxiety attacks* while at college at George Mason University in Virginia. He had been to see his doctor, and even a psychiatrist, but he could not shake it—no one seemed to be able to help him.

Back in Illinois, Kramer picked up his old journal and came across the quote from Mark's Gospel—*the healing of the leper.* He thought this passage might help Davis, so he sent it to him. This triggered an immediate response from his brother.

With choked-back emotion, Davis shared, "Kramer you won't believe what happened last night. I had a terrifying dream. When I looked down at my arms—they were covered with open sores and peeling skin. *I realized that I was a leper.* I awoke terrified. The experience was so real that I was afraid to even close my eyes again and risk that the nightmare might return. Then, the next day you sent me the Gospel reading about the healing of the leper."

Davis explained to Kramer that nothing special had happened earlier to trigger that dream. They both realized that this was a *God incident.* Then, Kramer shared with Davis that he had also felt that he was a leper when he first read Mark's Gospel passage four years earlier. Although the two brothers had both felt like the lepers of Mark's Gospel, Davis had actually experienced it in his nightmare.

Davis admitted to his brother that he had been slipping out of his relationship with God that he had so cherished earlier. Based on this dream, he was now committed to work on his prayer life and restore his relationship with God.

It took time, but Davis did completely recover from his anxiety attacks and now has been healed just as Jesus healed the leper when he called out to Him and Jesus said, *"I do will it. Be made clean."*

NOTE: Kramer has written a book titled, Fill Your Cup for Christ *to inspire Catholics of all ages to turn their life more fully to Christ through personal testimony, athletic experiences, and motivational stories.*

CHAPTER 25

Bishop Power

—◆—

Story from Matt Beardsley of the Shrine of St. Patrick's Oratory, in Green Bay, WI

The fervent prayer of a righteous person is very powerful.

JAMES 5:16

There are times when we turn to others for prayer to overcome some trial or need. Often that person is especially spiritual or close to God, but often it is a person that God has put in our life at the right time.

MATT WAS THE OLDEST OF three children. He had a younger brother and sister. His dad, David, was a civil engineer and his mom, Eileen, was a nurse. His mom and dad raised the children in a strong Catholic family with all three children attending Catholic school through high school.

His dad had been raised Baptist, but because they were married in a Catholic church, he had promised the priest that he would raise the children in the Catholic faith. When David made a promise, he intended to keep it fully. He not only attended Mass every Sunday with the family, but as time went by, he also was involved in the choir, Boy Scouts, and other activities in the parish.

Some people may have noticed that David never received Holy Communion. But in 2006, when the list of catechumens was announced at Sunday Mass, everyone was surprised to hear David's name among them. According to Matt, "There was an *audible gasp* heard throughout the church." Everyone thought David was already Catholic because he was so involved in the parish.

Ever since Matt was four or five, he always wanted to be *in radio*, so at a very young age he used to "play radio" in his imaginary studio in the basement. Later, a priest friend of the family introduced Matt to ham radio. Matt said, "After Catholic high school, I was mature enough to know that I wasn't mature enough to go to college and be on my own. So, I did the right thing, I joined the Navy to gain some discipline." This also gave Matt a chance to see the world: "I was on both sides of the world [England and Japan] before I was twenty."

In the US Navy, Matt followed his childhood dreams and worked as a radio operator. It was while in the Navy, in Thailand, that his belief in God and his Catholic faith blossomed in the most surprising place.

His Catholic chaplain had a rather unique way of looking out for his Catholic men. When the sailors were free to leave the ship and more than likely get into trouble, Father made a deal with them, "If you come with me [to the bar], I will buy." Surprisingly, during this time, the talk would often turn to their Catholic faith. It was one of these nights that Father explained the "Real Presence" to Matt in a way that made clear to him that Jesus was really present in the Eucharist. From that day forward, Matt was a different Catholic. He even considered becoming a priest.

He left the Navy when he was twenty-one and moved home. He enrolled in the local junior college in St. Louis, Missouri. While in the Navy, he had pursued his "radio dream," but at junior college he felt lost. *He was not happy.* This soon became evident to his dad, who challenged Matt to follow his childhood dreams and pursue a career in radio. With his dad's financial support, Matt enrolled in "broadcast school." This eventually led to work at CBS Radio. He was happy again because he was doing what he loved.

One day at work, he received a call from a CBS associate, who asked, "You're a devout Catholic, aren't you?" Matt responded, "Well, I go to Church every Sunday. I go to confession once a month and I pray all the time. . . . Yea, I guess I am a devout Catholic." Matt had never thought about it before, but before he could ask, "What this is about?" the friend hung up.

Within a few days, he got his explanation. Matt was contacted by Tony, who was starting a Catholic radio station in St. Louis. He needed a radio engineer who was a devout Catholic. Matt recognized this as a great opportunity to learn more about the radio business and do something for his faith, so without a lot of thought, he said, "Yes!" Once he settled into the new job, he realized how fulfilling it was, compared to working at CBS.

For three years he worked at the station, but eventually he felt that he needed more experience in other aspects of radio, so he went back to CBS. Within a year, Tony contacted Matt again for help. This time it was to help the Catholic station broadcast Sunday Mass at the famous St. Louis Cathedral. He realized that he would be able to do this job for Tony, while keeping his job at CBS, so he agreed to help.

It was during this work for Tony, on Holy Thursday 2004 that *it happened*. While he was walking into the church, he literally bumped into Archbishop Raymond Burke. When Matt realized who he had bumped into, he not only apologized to his excellency, but introduced himself and told the archbishop about his work with the Catholic radio station, though he had to explain that he no longer worked there.

"The archbishop looked me in the eye and asked why I had left Catholic radio." Matt explained that he had left to gain more experience at CBS, but he admitted how rewarding it had been to work for Catholic radio. The archbishop said, "I know a company, *Relevant Radio,* a Catholic radio company. I am very good friends with a lot of people who work there and a lot of the founders. Maybe you should look into them." Matt said that he had thought about it but had never pursued applying. With that they parted.

That night, Matt worked at CBS as a DJ playing music to an audience of 200,000 to 300,000 people. This is what Matt had dreamed about as a kid, but *something wasn't right*. The archbishop's words, "Why did you leave Catholic radio?" started to gnaw on him. That night, he checked the job postings and noticed that Relevant Radio had two job openings, so he sent in his resume and went to bed.

Two months later, he was contacted by Relevant Radio. He was interviewed several times but was never offered a job. A week later, Matt saw Archbishop Burke after evening Mass on the feast of Corpus Christi. The first thing the archbishop said was, "The last time we spoke I had mentioned Relevant Radio. Have you done anything about that? Did you ever contact Relevant Radio?"

Matt explained that he had been interviewed for a job there, but he had not heard back from them. The archbishop put his hand on Matt's shoulder and said, "I will pray for you tonight." He then made the sign of the cross on Matt's forehead.

The next morning, Matt received a call from Relevant Radio with a job offer. He gladly accepted.

Matt will always be grateful to the *chance meeting* with Archbishop Burke, who not only suggested that he contact *Relevant Radio*, but prayed that he would get the job.

God has a way of leading us in our search to do His will and in doing so, bringing us fulfillment and happiness.

NOTE: Matt has worked for Relevant Radio for the last sixteen years. He presently is the producer of the Morning Air show with John Harper and Glen Lewerenz, which airs at 5–9 a.m. Central Time. John Harper wrote the Introduction to this book.

CHAPTER 26

Divine Grace

—•—

Story from Deneen C. Seril of St. Angela's Catholic Church in Pacific Grove, CA

And whoever receives one child,
such as this in my name receives me.

MATTHEW 18:5

WHILE HER MOM DROVE, FIVE-YEAR-OLD Deneen played in the backseat of their car with the toys brought from home to entertain her.

It all had started with a heated disagreement between her mom and dad. Deneen was playing outside their house in California when her mom gathered her up with a promise of an ice cream cone—so off they went. When they left, her dad was nowhere in sight.

Deneen knew her mom was pregnant, so she wondered what was going on when they did not return home after the ice cream. Her mom just continued to drive in silence through the afternoon and even after it grew dark. These long stretches of silence were interrupted by some talk of the upcoming birth of Deneen's brother or sister. They spent the night in a motel.

The next day, Deneen learned that they were headed for Texas. Why Texas? Deneen never learned. Eventually, they found a place to live where Deneen's brother, John, was born. When Deneen was seven and John was about two, Deneen's mother turned over her kids to the state orphanage for adoption. She had tried, but raising two kids on her own without family support was too much for the young mother.

One day, Deneen and John were taken from the orphanage to the park, where they met a young couple and their teenage daughter. Much to Deneen's surprise, they were taken home by this couple. Within a week, Deneen found herself in a judge's chamber sitting in an immense leather chair faced with an important question for the seven-year-old.

The judge asked, "What is it that you want for yourself and your brother?"

She responded, "We should be together."

The judge told the couple that if they wanted the baby, they would have to take Deneen, too. Deneen was never discouraged—she took this just as a new experience. She liked her new family, and she was happy that she was with her brother.

Deneen learned that her new family was Catholic and that both parents had been raised on a farm with lots of brothers and sisters, so adding two children to their family was what they were used to in their upbringing. On Sundays, the family went to Church. The mother dressed them up in their best clothes. As a family, they would walk the two blocks to a little rural Catholic church. John was usually carried by his new father.

Within a month, something new was introduced to their regular Sunday church routine. Their new mom dressed Deneen and John in new white clothes, and instead of walking the two blocks to church, they all road in the family car. "I don't want you to get your clothes dirty," was their mom's explanation of why they were driving.

When she asked what was so special about that day, Deneen was told that they were going to be *baptized*.[1] Further questioning helped very little. She was told that baptism was a sacrament and she would have to come up with a saint's name[2] to take as her own. She could keep her own name but Deneen must also come up with a saint's name. Her new parents explained that they had chosen Mark for her brother's saint's name.

Her mom explained, "A saint is like your guardian angel." Of course, as a seven-year-old who had not been brought up in a Christian family, she didn't understand what an angel was. So that didn't help her understand what a saint was. More importantly, she didn't understand that baptism was how you became Catholic. Deneen's main concern was to come up with a name of a saint—nothing else mattered.

When it was time for the baptism, the parents, the godparents, Deneen and John were asked to come forward. Then the priest asked the parents, "What name are you giving your child?" They responded that she was old enough to answer that herself. The priest turned to Deneen and asked, "What is your name, little one?" She put her shoulders back and responded, "My name is Deneen Catherine."

Her parents and godparents asked together, "Who is Catherine?" All she could say was, "I have no idea, but she wanted me." Soon the baptism was over, and her godparents gave Deneen Catherine a porcelain statue of the Blessed Mother holding baby Jesus. (This statue is cherished by Deneen to this day.)

Over the years, Deneen and her brother grew and matured as part of their new family. They loved their mom and dad. After college, Deneen joined the Newman Club at Shepperd Air Force Base. This is where she met and fell in love with Frank, a young Air Force serviceman. After dating for some time, they were married. During their first year of marriage, Deneen bore their daughter, Jennifer.

During the next year, it became clear that something was *seriously wrong*—Deneen discovered that her husband was self-medicating on psychiatric prescriptions that he was stealing from work. After work, he would go into his room and instruct Deneen to leave him alone and that's where he would isolate himself.

Deneen's life was in a crisis. She said, "I was very much alone."

She decided to take her baby and find a Catholic church in the area where she could make friends and find a life for herself and her daughter. "I just wanted to find people we could enjoy and be with." She joined a youth group who was involved with a national movement called *Up with People*. God rushed back into her life through this wonderful, spirited movement. Remarkably, she was able to travel and participate in the performances. *She had found joy in her life again.*

Over the next few months, she not only grew close to the members of the group, but she also became close to the parish priest that worked with *Up with People*. One day, the priest asked about her life at home, only to discover the awful situation in which Deneen was living. He said, "God lives in the grace of our lives when He is present in our relationships."

God was not present in their marital relationship. *There was no relationship.* Her priest went on to point out that Deneen's duty was to her daughter and herself. Deneen decided to divorce her husband. For the next five years, she remained with *Up with People*. She had a job at the Department of Defense to support her child. "Life was not easy, but I managed just fine."

When Jennifer was almost six, Deneen met Richard at work. After dating for some time, they married. Their first decision as a couple was where should they live—close to Deneen's parents in Texas or near his family in Monterey, California. *Monterey won out.*

In Monterey they were blessed with three more children (Carrie, Sasha, and Richard). They attended the youth Mass at St. Angela's Catholic Church that helped the children to participate and feel part of the service.

When Deneen's children were five, seven, nine, and sixteen years old, Deneen and her husband had a basic disagreement about how to spend Friday evenings. Deneen wanted to grab some fast food and go to the beach to play and watch the sunset. Richard wanted to go for "Happy Hour" with friends from work. Neither parent would compromise, so they each did their own thing—Deneen and the kids, and Richard with his friends. This separation on Fridays continued for weeks.

Deneen had no idea that *her husband's midlife crisis was about to hit the family.* Then, one night after the children were asleep, Richard told her that he was leaving her for another woman and moving to Texas.

Deneen was devastated.

That night, Deneen stood in the kitchen *alone.* She was overcome with grief and fear by the impact of Richard's departure. She fell back against the wall and slid down to the floor as she lifted her arms to God and cried out for help: "I can't do this myself. If you're really there, I need you now . . . I can't do this alone!" In that moment, Deneen said, "I literally felt washed with a beautiful light of *divine grace*, moving through and around me."

God was with her and would help her through this new crisis. *"I will never forsake you or abandon you." (Hebrews 13:5)*

The next day, Deneen gathered the family together for a *heart to heart talk.* She told the kids, "Your father has left us, but we are not alone. God is with us. We're going to do this together and have a good time doing it because laughter is the best healing we can have."

NOTE: Deneen went on to raise her four children in the Catholic faith. I found Deneen a happy and amazingly upbeat woman who still works. She has spent years in supporting St. Angela's by working with the youth who are in the RCIA program.[3] God never abandoned her.

---

[1] Baptism is the basis of the whole Christian life, the gateway to life in the Spirit and the door that gives access to the other sacraments. Through baptism, we are freed from sin and reborn as sons and daughters of God; we become members of Christ, are incorporated into the Church and become sharers in her mission: "Baptism is the sacrament of regeneration through water in the word." (Source: *The Catechism of the Catholic Church*, Article 1, 1213.)

[2] Using the name of *a saint* is not normally part of baptism; perhaps confirmation was also part of the ceremony, in which the candidate does take the name of a saint.

[3] RCIA (The Rite of Christian Initiation of Adults) is a process developed by the Catholic Church for prospective converts to Catholicism who are above the age of infant baptism. Candidates are introduced to aspects of Catholic beliefs and practices over a six-month or longer period of weekly small-group meetings with other interested prospective converts, as well as members of the parish who act as sponsors. Guest speakers are often local priests or the pastor of the parish. During this period, close friendships are built that provide a sense of community and welcoming, as well as period of openness to learn about the Catholic Church.

CHAPTER 27

I Am with You Always

———•———

Story from Catherine Norris of Our Lady of Mt. Carmel
Catholic Church, Carmel Valley, California

And behold, I am with you always,
until the end of the age.

MATTHEW 28:20

C ATHERINE WAS BORN IN ATLANTA, Georgia, the second
oldest of four children. They all attended Catholic
schools through high school. In Atlanta, confirmation
was received at nine years old. This may explain Catherine's
story, because the Holy Spirit was active early in her life.

Catherine went to Christ the King Catholic Grammar School
followed by Marist School (high school), where she was part
of the third year in which girls could attend in the previously
all-boys military school. When the switch-over took place, the
school not only added girls to the school, but they dropped
the military aspect as well.

The Marist order of priests, brothers, and nuns teach at the school. Catherine said, "I had just an outstanding experience there and I made many friends, and I am still kept in contact with five of them monthly."

The statement of the Marist School is as follows: "Our spirituality is marked by a profound experience of God's abiding presence and love, by trust in God, by a deep personal love of Jesus and His Gospel, by community living in a family spirit, and by a humility expressed through simplicity."

When you meet Catherine, you can see the influence of the Marist School on her life.

Catherine continued her education at Boston College, where she was in the Physical Therapy program. When she was eighteen and still a freshman, she received a devastating phone call from her mother. She said to Catherine, "Are you sitting down?" She then went on to tell Catherine that her twenty-five-year-old sister, Mary Carroll, had died of a massive pulmonary embolism as a result of surgery on her knee.

The family was devastated. It was their strong faith that pulled them through that tragedy. "Going back to school after the funeral was one of the toughest things I have ever done. I know that if it weren't for my faith, I would not have been able to do it."

It was years later as a physical therapist that she was able to share the healing power that she had been taught at Boston

College and integrate it with her profound love and trust in God. Therapy combined with prayer became a way of life for Catherine. "I used to tell the kids in my religious education class that the rosary is a 'nuclear bomb' of prayer."

The rosary became a form of prayer that she often turns to, especially when times are tough. "When I ask Mary to plead my cause, I am telling you that God without fail answers me every single time. When I say the rosary, there are at least fifty to sixty people I remember by name. I have watched the healing happen in their lives and I know it is because Mary pleaded my cause and God answered my prayer."

It is with this confidence that Catherine approaches her ministry of healing of both body and spirit.

Praise God!

Note: Catherine is a lector at Our Lady of Mount Carmel and owns her physical therapy practice.

CHAPTER 28

Mighty Angels

———•—•———

Story from Carol Anger of St. Andrew Catholic Church, Cape
Coral, Florida

Take your place, stand firm, and see
how the Lord will be with you.

2 CHRONICLES 20:17

CAROL WAS BORN IN SOUTH Milwaukee, Wisconsin.
Her mom, Arlene, played a major role in her life. She
made sure that Carol and her two brothers had a strong
Catholic education.

When she was at St. Adalbert's Catholic grammar school, the
school principal, a Franciscan sister, gathered all the girls into
the school hall and asked them, "Who wants to go to heaven?"
Carol was quick to raise her hand with all her classmates. The
sister explained that the Blessed Virgin Mary wanted people
to attended Mass on the first Saturday of the month for three

consecutive Saturdays, pray the rosary, receive the Eucharist, and go to confession. Mary said that she promises to bring those who honor these requests by bringing their souls to heaven on the first Saturday of the month.

This message had a major effect on Carol and she did her best to meet those requirements and today still attends Mass on Saturdays.

Carol enjoyed her Catholic education through high school, but then she slipped away from the Church for ten years, because of a misunderstanding with God. While she struggled with wanting to return to the Church, she hesitated. Then one day, she received something in the mail that included a passage from the 23rd Psalm—"something just clicked."

She asked God for help, "You know that I have been away for a long time, and I need to come back to You. But I don't have any friends that are Catholic . . . I'm lost. So, He set me up with friends that are truly religious, including a priest, Fr. Peter Mary Rookey, O.S.M."

God honored her request, but instead of bringing just one person to help her return, He brought three.

Carol was soon not only back to Church, but was also involved in pilgrimages to Medjugorje and other religious sites. She had reestablished her relationship with God, so it was not surprising that she continued to see God's hand in her life and the lives of her family even to this day.

While in her early fifties, Carol's mom, Arlene, was diagnosed with stage-four colon cancer in 2005. Then, in 2006, she was diagnosed with 95 percent blockage of her carotid artery,[1] but it was too close to her brain for them to operate on it. The doctor said, "If we go in there, you might end up paralyzed."

Her life was at risk, but they could not do anything to help her.

Carol went to her friend Fr. Peter. He celebrated Mass and offered it for her mother; he prayed over her, and then took her to the Basilica of Our Lady of Sorrows in Chicago to the area behind the altar where there are relics of saints, including St. Peregrine, the patron of those suffering from cancer. He prayed that the saints would intercede for her.

Within a week, they received a call from the hospital telling them that they had a possible medical procedure, "strictly experimental," that might save her life. Arlene said, "Let's go for it, otherwise I am going to die." And it worked; the artery was opened without any adverse results.

Then in 2007, Carol received a call telling her to come quickly because Arlene was in the ICU. She was not doing well, and she was in a lot of pain. The doctors said that she had become septic,[2] the same condition that had taken Carol's grandmother years earlier. Carol, her husband, Don, and her young son, Andrew, packed their bags and went to northern Wisconsin to be with Arlene.

Carol said, "Upon arriving at the hospital, I went into the hospital chapel with tears streaming down my eyes while silently praying. I told Jesus that I was mentally and physically exhausted. He had just taken my father to heaven, *I asked Him not take my mother too.*

"Lord, everything You asked of me, I have done. I taught the children at my son's Catholic school about the Blessed Virgin Mary, Lourdes, Fatima, and the Eucharistic miracle at Luciano, and your Real Presence in the Eucharist.

"Lord, if I go into my mother's ICU room, I will either cry hysterically or pass out on the floor. You alone know my mental and physical exhaustion. Jesus, please send me two big, strong guardian angels to hold me up upon entering her room.

"Before pressing the button to enter the ICU unit, I wiped away my tears, put on my calm-in-control face, and asked Jesus to send me His two big, strong guardian angels and have them grab me under my arms and hold me up and give me strength.

"When I entered my mother's room, her eyes lit up and the biggest smile came upon her face. The first words that came out of her mouth were: 'You have two Big, Bright, Beautiful Guardian Angels with you. They are so big, bright, and beautiful. Each one is holding you up by your arms.' At that very moment, my heart was filled with joy; Jesus had heard me and answered my prayers."

Praise God!

NOTE: Arlene is still alive today enjoying life now fourteen years later.

———•———

[1] The carotid arteries are major blood vessels in the neck that supply blood to the brain, neck, and face.

[2] Sepsis is a potentially life-threatening condition that occurs when the body's response to an infection damages its own tissues. When the infection-fighting processes turn on the body, they cause organs to function poorly and abnormally. Sepsis may progress to septic shock. This is a dramatic drop in blood pressure that can lead to severe organ problems and death. Early treatment with antibiotics and intravenous fluids improves chances for survival.

ACKNOWLEDGMENTS

I AM ESPECIALLY GRATEFUL TO MY wife, Lois, who spent hours doing the initial proofing of this document and being a loving critic. I am also extremely indebted to Ann Aubrey Hanson for the final editing and her many helpful comments.

Thanks also to my attorney brother, Bob, for advising me on all the copyright and other legal issues that relate to using other people's stories in my book, and to my son Stephen who created the cover design of the book.

I also owe a great deal of thanks to John Harper, the host of *Morning Air*, for writing the *Introduction* and for his endorsement of the book and his encouraging words on his show. Before he wrote the *Introduction*, he read all three books.

I am indebted to my friend William Cather Hook, who allowed me to use his painting, *Red Sky*© for the cover of this book.

I also want to thank all those parishioners who were so enthusiastic in purchasing the *GOD Incidents* series after Mass during the past years. It was their overwhelming positive response that encouraged me to write *GOD Incidents III*.

I want to thank the Most Reverend Daniel E. Garcia, DD, Bishop of the Diocese of Monterey, for giving me permission to sell this book at the churches in the Diocese of Monterey to raise money for the diocesan schools and religious formation programs of the parishes.

Finally, I especially need to thank all the storytellers who were willing to share their "God incidents" with me. This was their chance to acknowledge and thank God for acting in their lives in a powerful way. Without these storytellers and their amazing stories, this book would not have been possible.

SHARE YOUR GOD INCIDENT

I HAVE BEEN VERY BLESSED TO have been allowed to hear these "God incident" stories firsthand and to meet the storytellers. The more I hear new stories, the more I am amazed at how much God loves us. We are not isolated or left to fend for ourselves. God cares for us, as His children. This is especially evident when you read these stories.

I have been especially moved by the response from parishioners where I have sold books after Mass to support the parish's religious formation programs (CCD, Confirmation, and RCIA). I witness a hunger to read these true stories. I only wish I could reach more people with stories of God's love for mankind.

If you want to share your own God incident story send me an email to *ShareGodIncidents@gmail.com. You don't have to write your story*, just send me an email stating you want to share your story. I will contact you and set up a time for a phone interview. (Phone interviews can work very well to hear your

God incident story. I will write your story, and I will send you a copy for your review.) Once the book is published, you will receive a free book that includes your story.

So, if you want to see your story in *GOD Incidents IV,* send me an email and I will contact you.

Thomas R. Jukes

ABOUT THE AUTHOR

———•———

Thomas R. Lukes is a lifelong Catholic and a retired architect. As an architect, he worked on many church-related and school projects. When he was thirty, he had a special encounter[1] with God that motivated him to live his life for God while serving his church. Today, he serves as lector and eucharistic minister at his parish.

For five years, he served as lay director of the Cursillo movement in Monterey, California, and was editor of the Cursillo newsletter, which he renamed *Rekindle*. In 2011, Lukes was part of Bishop Richard Garcia's committee to bring *Immaculate Heart Radio*® to the Monterey Bay area. On Oct 14, 2016, *Immaculate Heart Radio* merged with *Relevant Radio*® and is a great source of Catholic teaching for the layman of the Church.

He has appeared numerous times on *Relevant Radio's Morning Air* and *The Drew Mariani Show*. His first book, *GOD Incidents—True Stories of God Working in the Lives of Catholics,* was used as a Pledge Drive gift, so a total of 1,575 listeners at Relevant Radio received a copy of the book.

Proceeds from all three books go to support Catholic religious formation in the Diocese of Monterey.

Lukes and his wife, Lois, have three sons and six grandchildren. In his retirement, Lukes enjoys daily Mass, reading, and playing golf—as well as interviewing storytellers and writing about their "God incidents."

---

[1] See the author's first book, *GOD Incidents—True Stories of God Working in the Lives of Catholics*, Chapter 18, "Our Encounter."

Red Sky © William Cather Hook 2004

COVER STORY

William Cather Hook is a friend of the mine who allowed me to use his painting entitled *Red Sky* as the cover for this third book.

Each summer for twenty years, William Hook taught painting at the Fechin Institute in San Cristobal, New Mexico, which is a little north of Taos. Will tells the story that this sunset was noticed by his students during dinner, and everyone rushed outside with cameras in hand to capture this spectacular sunset. Will said that his resulting photograph did not capture the rich colors, but fortunately, he was able to duplicate them in this wonderful image.

"For three decades, the signature 'W. C. Hook' has connoted dynamic design, saturated color, and compelling brushwork. William Cather Hook's ability to straddle the border between pictorial illusion and pure paint, between traditionalism and modernism, has won him collectors worldwide.

"Less known about this versatile colorist is the breadth of his subject matter. Through his paintings and observations, Hook guides the reader on a journey that includes the back roads of northern New Mexico, the high country of the Colorado Rockies and Sangre de Cristos, and California's Route 1 coastline and Central Valley. The Sonoran Desert, English and Italian countryside, and garden still lifes are also the subjects of this master of acrylics, whose vision is inviting, vibrant, and infused with radiant light." (Source: Susan Hallsten McGarry author of *William Cather Hook: A Retrospective*)

For more of Hook's work, see https://www.williamhook.net.

THE *GOD INCIDENTS* BOOK SERIES

BOOK I

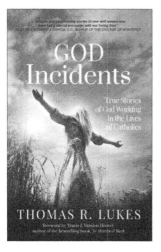

The author explains in the Preface how the book series first came about with God's direction and explains who are the storytellers.

GOD Incidents provides a collection of stories that cover a range of topics showing evidence of God's hand in our daily lives.

"Thomas describes well the intimate and transforming stories of men and women who have had a special encounter with our loving God."—Most Reverend Richard J. Garcia, D.D., Bishop of the Diocese of Monterey

Based on true stories as told to the author, *GOD Incidents* shows that not everything is a coincidence; if you look closely, you may just see God showing up in your life.

BOOK II

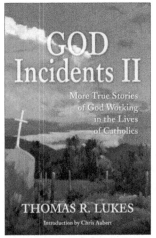

GOD Incidents II includes a variety of stories: miraculous healings, an angel's intersession, a near-death experience, a Marian apparition, and many more stories.

"If you're looking for hope and tangible assurance that God knows your situation and will not abandon you, then GOD Incidents II is a must read.

"It will inspire you, life you up, and remind you that all things are possible with God!"—Drew Mariani, *Relevant Radio*® Host

The people in these stories show their willingness to trust God, as they went through transformational experiences that strengthened their faith and encouraged them to continue their walk with the Lord.

In a world that has grown apart from God, the stories in *GOD Incidents II* will help us to see God as a caring and loving father.

ATTENTION: To order books, type in

relevantradio.com/truestories

in the search bar.

Made in the USA
Monee, IL
15 July 2021

72973556R00115